MAINSTREAMING:
Controversy
and
Consensus

Edited by
Patrick A. O'Donnell
and Robert H. Bradfield

Academic Therapy Publications
San Rafael, California 94901

© *Copyright 1976*
Academic Therapy Publications
1539 Fourth Street
San Rafael, California 94901

Tests, books and materials
for and about the learning disabled

All rights reserved.
This book, or parts thereof,
may not be reproduced
in any form
without permission
from the publisher.

Each author's words are
his own and do not necessarily
reflect the point of view
of the editors. Each author
has been encouraged to
present his own
perspective and viewpoint.

> Library of Congress Cataloging in Publication Data
> Main entry under title:
> Mainstreaming.
>
>   1. Handicapped children—Education—United States. 2. Handicapped children—Law and legislation—United States. I. O'Donnell, Patrick A. II. Bradfield, Robert H.
> LC4031.M28   371.9'0973   76-41283
> ISBN 0-87879-158-2

This book was set in IBM
Press Roman 11 point medium, italic,
and bold type. Display faces
were Varityper 30 point and
18 point Bodoni bold. The paper used
was 60 pound Spring Forge Offset for the text;
10 point CIS for the cover.

Printed in the
United States of America

Contents

Introduction, by Patrick A. O'Donnell 5

Chapter 1
Special Education: Legal Aspects,
by Richard Bancroft 11

Chapter 2
What Research Tells Us about Mainstreaming,
by Barbara Keogh 25

Chapter 3
Mainstreaming: Historical Perspectives,
by Maynard Reynolds 39

Chapter 4
Mainstreaming: Assessment Issues,
by Asa G. Hilliard 55

Chapter 5
*The IQ Test and Classification: An Inherently
Harmful Situation,* by Armando M. Menocal, III........71

Chapter 6
*Placement in Special Classes:
The Defendant's Viewpoint, the* Larry P. *Case,*
by Joanne Condas Rabin..........................79

Chapter 7
Emerging Placement Alternatives: Implications for Teacher-Training Programs,
by Leo Cain. 89

Chapter 8
The Houston Plan: A Program that Works,
by Charles Meisgeier 99

Chapter 9
Special Education in Vermont: The Consulting Teacher Approach, by Hugh McKenzie 115

Chapter 10
How to Fail in Mainstreaming without Really Trying,
by Robert H. Bradfield 129

Chapter 11
Mainstreaming: Some Basis for Caution,
by Robert Stannard. 141

About the Authors 151

Introduction

Professional and parental interest in the mainstreaming of handicapped children has increased dramatically in the past few years. In this book the authors have traced some of the implications for teacher training and for programing in the schools. Forces which are mandating that schools examine the concept and its implications, as well as forces which may determine the success or failure of the experiment, are discussed in depth in this book.

In Chapter 1, Richard Bancroft documents the entry of the courts and legal system into education. Starting with *Brown* v. *Board of Education* and recently with the *Larry P.* case, the courts have taken an increasingly active role in the development of educational policy.* Bancroft traces the past uses of litigation as a means for solving educational problems. He points out some of the limits of litigation as a means for improving education programs. In particular, he defines key legal concepts which are exerting a substantial influence on special education at the present time. Among

---

* *Larry P.* v. *Wilson Riles* 343 F. Supp. 1306 (N.D. Cal. 1972). Action involving the right to be free from inappropriate educational classification, labeling, and placement. A preliminary injunction has been entered to the effect that no black pupil may be placed in EMR classes on the basis of criteria which rely primarily on the results of IQ tests if the consequence of the use of such tests is racial imbalance in the composition of EMR classes. —From the President's Committee on Mental Retardation (Department of Health, Education, and Welfare, October 1974): 75-2107: 32-33.

these concepts are *due process, equal protection,* and *right to education.* Of special importance may be the question raised regarding whether we ought to continue to look toward the courts for solutions to what are essentially educational questions.

Barbara Keogh reviews the research on the effects of mainstreaming on children previously assigned to special education classes in Chapter 2. As pointed out by the author, the research is scant and inconclusive. She reviews the efforts in California to mainstream former special education pupils through the Educable Mentally Retarded Transition (EMRT) program. Keogh relates the mainstreaming effort to the current doctrine of placement in the "least restrictive alternative." Among the important questions rasied by Keogh is the issue of seeking placement for handicapped children which proves effective for both the children formerly enrolled in special education classes and for children currently enrolled in regular classes.

Maynard Reynolds recounts a brief history of special education placement, particularly aspects which relate to contemporary mainstreaming efforts in Chapter 3. He describes early programs concentrated primarily in residential schools and the later community-based programs. He views them as leading to the current period, which he characterizes as an effort to achieve greater inclusion and integration. Reynolds has provided an enlightening context for current issues and trends.

Asa Hilliard carefully defines many of the issues related to the assessment and placement of handicapped children in Chapter 4. The issues provide background for the current trend toward mainstreaming. He traces, briefly, the history of intelligence testing in this country and the uses and misuses which have been made of standardized instruments. He places some current ideas regarding intelligence into historical perspective. Perhaps most important, Hilliard illustrates problems of existing intelligence tests as they relate to the various subcultures in this country. Hilliard's comments are particularly relevant at this time in view of the conditions established in PL 94-142* which pro-

---

*Public Law 94-142 [Education for all Handicapped Children Act] established a formula in which the federal government makes a commitment to say a gradually-escalating percentage of the National Average Expenditure per public

hibit use of culturally biased tests for assessment and placement of handicapped children.

In Chapter 5, Armando Menocal describes briefly the the plantiff's viewpoint in the pivotal *Larry P.* case. Menocal raises questions similar to those raised by Hilliard about inappropriate assessment. He again points out the various racial issues which appear to have become relevant with regard to intelligence testing. Menocal provides a succinct but enlightening description of the plaintiff's viewpoint regarding inappropriate assessment, placement based on that assessment, and the eventual effects of misplacement.

Joanne Condas Rabin, the attorney for the state of California in the *Larry P.* case, documents some of the impact of the *Larry P.* decision on special education programs and the children who were represented in the case in Chapter 6. While she does not defend the misuse of intelligence tests, she seriously questions the wisdom of abandoning all use of the instruments at this time. She suggests ways that the IQ test might be used more judiciously. Rabin also questions whether the courtroom is the appropriate forum for raising the kinds of questions that were raised by the *Larry P.* case.

In Chapter 7, Leo Cain discusses the history of credential legislation in the state of California, particularly as it relates to current efforts to mainstream handicapped children. He suggests some of the relationships between placement alternatives in the schools and teacher training programs. He traces the relationship between the California Master Plan for Special Education and existing credential policies. Cain suggests some directions for change in preservice teacher training programs if mainstreaming is to become a viable placement policy. Among the needs are teachers with more generic training and better-trained regular classroom teachers.

In Chapter 8, Charles Meisgeier describes a successful mainstreaming program in Houston. The approach used in that community is best described as a responsive delivery

school child times the number of handicapped children being served in the school district of each State in the Nation. That percentage will escalate on a yearly basis until 1982 when it will become permanent for the percent for that year and all subsequent years. (Overview developed for the Council for Exceptional Children.)

system which utilized a systems approach to the delivery of service. According to Meisgeier, the approach more creatively used existing resources to improve the level of instruction for all children. Of no small importance was the effort to establish and maintain emphasis on changing fundamentals rather than symptoms. As with Cain, Meisgeier supports the notion of a need for massive reeducation of regular teachers. He suggests that we must impact teachers, parents and funding agencies. Meisgeier provides a very enlightening discussion of a large scale mainstreaming effort.

Hugh McKenzie provides a very helpful description of the *consulting teacher model* which was developed in the state of Vermont in Chapter 9. The model was characterized by planning which integrated teacher training and programing in the schools. The model was a further attempt to deal with economic realities. The model incorporated high levels of accountability and provided for the involvement of many varied professionals in the schools. The model incorporates substantial parent participation and involvement and assures due process for placement and programing.

Based upon his experience with mainstreaming efforts in school districts, Robert Bradfield suggests some criteria which must be considered for successful mainstreaming in Chapter 10. He questions the artificial boundaries between disciplines which have existed within teacher training institutions and in public school programs. He emphasizes the need for broad involvement in the process. Bradfield's cautions provide some refreshing and necessary balance.

In Chapter 11, Robert Stannard relates his actual and personal experience with mainstream efforts in a school district. He suggests some of the possible losses that could occur with overly optimistic and rapid movement into mainstreaming. He cites frequent reactions of teachers and parents to the concept and generally reflects a segment of the educational community that has not been heard from too frequently with regard to this issue. As with Bradfield, Stannard raises questions which are absolutely critical if mainstreaming is not to become a concept which was tried and found wanting and unworkable.

P.A.O.
July 7, 1976

CHAPTER 1

Special Education:

Legal Aspects

Richard Bancroft

Concern for the legal rights of the handicapped is burgeoning across the country. This concern is supported by the American Bar Association, by state and local bar associations. The matter of legal education is coming to the fore. Our San Francisco Bar Association president has been advocating that law indeed be taught in the grammar schools, the junior high schools, and the high schools. I am not only an advocate of courses such as these, but also an advocate of compulsory courses on the legal rights of the handicapped in all schools and universities that dedicate themselves to the teaching profession. These courses can provide sinews for the kind of strength needed to deal with a complex world. It is my experience that there is an enormous lack of information regarding the basic tools necessary for functioning in our society, particularly legal matters that seem to permeate the atmosphere. I hope that perhaps, as I proceed, it will become clear that there is need for an extension of this kind of education.

I take my text from a decision of the United States Supreme Court in 1954, *Brown* v. *Board of Education,* a decision that established the principle that segregation of black children in public school education irrespective of the equality or asserted equality of tangible and material factors is a violation of the equal protection clause of the

Constitution. The significance of this case to me in the field of education is contained within some very specific language that I think ought to be a bible for all educators. This language is far broader than the issues in the case, far broader than the concerns of black persons, far broader indeed than the problems of exceptional persons. It extends to the entire field of education and could serve very well as a basis for an entire quarter's or semester's discussion. The words are as follows:

> Today, education is perhaps the most important function of state and local governments. Compulsory school attendance laws and the great expenditures for education both demonstrate our recognition of the importance of education in our democratic society. It is required in the performance of our most basic public responsibilities, even service in the armed forces. It is the very foundation of good citizenship. Today it is a principal instrument in awakening the child to cultural values, in preparing him for later professional training, and in helping him to adjust normally to his environment. In these days, it is doubtful that any child may reasonably be expected to succeed in life if he is denied the opportunity of an education.

Any professor might have written those words. Any lawyer might have written those words. Their impact would have been slight. But those words, deliberately subscribed to by unanimous vote of the United States Supreme Court, because of the tremendous importance of judicial precedent are words that will continue to have an all-pervading significance in the field of education. And it is from those words that most of the recent developments in the law, insofar as the exceptional child or adult is concerned, have come.

Underlying that decision and other decisions in the field are twin doctrines of great significance. The first is the doctrine of "due process of law." The second is "equal protection of law." Due process of law is covered in those portions of the Fifth Amendment and the Fourteenth Amendment to the Constitution which requires that our governments, state and Federal, accord to individuals their rights, their liberties, their freedoms, and justice. Their just desserts are guaranteed by the due process clause of these amendments. It means reasonableness, it means fairness. It means a lack of deprivation for persons who may be confined—as in mental hospitals, as in institutions, as in jails, as in schools. It means the right of free speech, the right of assembly, the right of peaceable worship. The First Amendment rights and all other constitutional rights coalesce within the language of the due process clauses. It means that our government must act fairly in order not to harm the individual or groups of persons within our society. This is called "substantive due process."

To guarantee substantive due process, there is another aspect of due process called "procedural due process." Procedural due process requires fair procedure. It requires that the means by which any one citizen or any group of citizens are deprived of life, liberty, or property be fair and that they be reasonable, requiring notice, hearing, attorney representation, the right to answer charges, etc. These rights were guaranteed by the Magna Carta originally, eventually written into our Constitution, and later spelled out in thousands of decisions in our courts throughout the country.

These twin doctrines have been at the very foundation of the total field of law called civil rights and civil liberties. Civil rights involving the rights of minorities—black minorities, Asian minorities, American Indian minorities, political minorities and religious and other minorities—have been at the foundation of our laws relating to crime and the rights of criminals who are confined. They have been at the foundation of developments in the field of mental health and, most recently, in the field of exceptional children. Without these two doctrines we would have no basis for appealing to the original concept of justice upon which our nation was founded.

I come immediately into the field of exceptional persons to trace very briefly some history with respect to court cases.

First, I want to deal with the doctrine of "right to treatment," which parallels, supports, and amplfies the significance of the "right to education" I'll address shortly. In 1946 Dr. Morton Birnbaum, an attorney and a physician, wrote an article entitled "The Right to Treatment" for the

13

American Bar Association Journal. He is also an educator now at the forefront of the fight for the rights of exceptional persons. That article provided the basis for review by lawyers and judges and special educators all over the country, and it is the acknowledged precursor of many very important decisions of the courts, the first being *Rouse* v. *Cameron.* I do not mean the first in time; I mean the first and foremost in terms of significance in this field. This case involved the habeas corpus petition of a person found not guilty by reason of insanity in a District of Columbia court. He was confined in an institution, where, he later claimed through his attorneys, he was not receiving proper treatment. Therefore, he asked that he be released. His contention was that adequacy of treatment was the only basis that could be used for his confinement. The District of Columbia court held in those circumstances that there was proper use of the habeas corpus petition, that it was a valid way for a person confined in an institution to test not only whether he should be released but also the question of adequacy of treatment.

In the Rouse opinion, there was a suggestion that a number of constitutional safeguards were being overlooked in any situation in which confinement did not result in treatment and/or rehabilitation.

Then came the case of *Nason* v. *Bridgewater* in Massachusetts in 1968, two years after *Rouse* v. *Cameron,* in which a similar question was brought before the court. This case went all the way to the Massachusetts State Supreme Court. The court, basing its conclusion on Massachusetts statutes, found that adequate treatment was not being provided for the person who had been confined after having pleaded not guilty by reason of insanity and having been found not guilty by reason of insanity but who was nevertheless committed to a mental institution called Bridgewater in the state of Massachusetts. Again, the Supreme Court of that state took note of the possible consitutional violations involved in having an individual in a situation where he was merely being warehoused, where he was merely being held in custody without any concern for his advance or progress.

Then came the landmark decision of *Wyatt* v. *Stickney,* since appealed to the U. S. Court of Appeals under the name *Wyatt* v. *Adderholt,* with a decision affirming the decision of the lower court. This case involved a class-action suit against Alabama hospitals which had, among their patients, mentally retarded persons as well as geriatric patients who were being confined under circumstances where the claim was that the treatment was inhumane, lower than standards generally accepted by health professionals. The court held for the plaintiffs, the members of the class in this case, and stated three basic principles of treatment, which are now being adopted by the courts throughout the country: first, a humane psychological and physical environment; second, a qualified staff in numbers sufficient to administer adequate treatment; and third, individualized treatment plans.

Pay particular attention to the language—"individualized treatment plans"—and make the transition between the "right to treatment" in mental hospitals and similar institutions and the "right to individualized education" in the fields of general and special education. The oft-quoted language of the Wyatt case judge is as follows:

"Absent treatment, the hospital is transformed into a penitentiary."

The Wyatt case is an absolute blockbuster of a judicial decision within the field of special education. It is the kind of case where the court undertook to monitor the state system. A Federal District Court judge, a little judge in Alabama named Johnson, was able to express all of his feelings about the needs in these hospitals for exceptional persons, in language which is trenchant, sharp, and revealing, and which is based primarily on the expert testimony of special educators, physicians and mental-health professionals who know how these institutions should operate and how the individuals within them should be dealt with. In the case of *Wyatt* v. *Stickney,* Judge Johnson said that lack of money in the state of Alabama could be no excuse for a failure to maintain adequate and proper conditions, going to the extent of threatening that, if necessary, he could arrange for the sale of the property on which the hospital stood to provide proper treatment.

Then there is the case of *Donaldson* v. *O'Connor,* ultimately a Supreme Court decision, lawsuit by an individual. In this case, a damage award was upheld against the superintendent of a state hospital as well as a physician on the staff for failure to provide the kind of treatment in that institution that would accord with minimal and generally accepted standards in that community. I will refer to this case later when we come to discuss accountability, but it is significant in indicating that the law courts are able to deal with situations involving groups of citizens in institutions not only when the attack is directed against the system but also when the attack is directed upon individuals who fail to live up to professional standards.

Out of these cases comes a doctrine that is equally applicable to special education—the "least restrictive alternative" or the "least restrictive setting." To see that doctrine exemplified, you may look at the case of *Lake* v. *Cameron*, which has to do with a sixty-year-old woman who was simply wandering the streets of the District of Columbia without harm to anyone and thereafter committed involuntarily to St. Elizabeth's Hospital in Washington, D.C. The court concluded that that was the most severe kind of treatment that she could have been accorded and that she should have been placed in the "least restrictive setting." In this case, the least restrictive setting would, of course, be outpatient care, thereafter foster care, thereafter half-way houses, then day hospitals, then nursing homes, all the way to full-time hospitals. According to the teaching of the Wyatt case, the degree of restriction depends upon the severity of the problem and the skillful use of the techniques in the field. That's the right to treatment in a nutshell. It is expanding; it is growing rapidly. Lawyers and organizations for special persons throughout the country are pushing, of course, to develop more and more decisions in the field. As these decisions are rendered, they will particularize what are appropriate standards for treatment for systems as well as for individuals who are the providers of services both inside and outside the sytems.

To come back, then, to the field of the right to education, *Brown* v. *Board of Education* stands squarely at the bottom of all the cases that have been decided. I will run through a number of the most significant cases in the field; but there are hundreds and hundreds more that I haven't space to mention. Ramifications of these decisions have sweeping, broad implications. In the case of *Hobson* v.

Hansen in 1967 in the District of Columbia, the tracking system was outlawed, a very distinctive case relying very heavily on the case of *Brown* v. *Board of Education.* And then there is the case in 1971 of *PARC* v. *Pennsylvania* (Pennsylvania Association for the Retarded against the Commonwealth of Pennsylvania). It was decided, by a consent decree, that Pennsylvania laws, effectively excluding the mentally retarded from the system of education in Pennsylvania, were unconstitutional and in violation of the due process and equal protection clauses of the Constitution. This was the first and precedent-setting case establishing by class action that the right to education for those previously excluded or denied access could be established by a court on the broad foundation of the Constitution. Since that time, of course, cases have been filed all over the country, notably in Maryland, New York, North Carolina, and California.

In the District of Columbia, there was an even more significant case, though not the key case that started the trend: *Mills* v. *Board of Education of the District of Columbia.* One of the reasons this case is distinctive is that it did not involve a consent decree. That is to say, the parties themselves did not simply agree between themselves and have the judge sign the decree; rather they contested it all the way. So the decision of Judge Waddie, who decided this case, became what lawyers regard as a significant, meaningful legal precedent, and it was not reversed or overturned by any other court.

Not only does it stand as the law of the District of Columbia, it really stands in effect as the law of the land in Federal courts and jurisdictions throughout the United States. It is also distinctive because *Mills* v. *Board of Education* affected not just the mentally retarded but all exceptional persons and took special note of the situation of the poor.

In both the PARC and Mills cases, there were detailed, refined descriptions of what due porcess means in school settings with respect to assessment, classifications, assignments, the rights of parents, the right to representation, access to records, impartial hearing officers, etc.–the full panoply of due-process rights. These rights may be needlessly frightening to those who automatically transfer the

17

requirements of those cases to many of the situations that will be faced in mainstreaming in the state of California and other parts of the country.

I should mention the San Francisco case of *In re Larry P.*, decided by Judge Peckham, a class-action suit in which the City of San Francisco was enjoined from classifying black children as EMR children and placing them in EMR classes based upon IQ testing. This case was the beginning of a thorough examination—but merely the beginning—of the lack of validity of IQ testing for the purposes for which it has been used. It challenges our profession to come up with better testing methods and challenges us to do a great deal more with respect to the matters of classification and assessment.

Locally, the case of *Diana* v. *State Board of Education* deals with the language problems of Spanish-American children. And then there is a case that went all the way to the United States Supreme Court, *Lou* v. *Nichols*, dealing with bilingual instruction. The decision here requires that in effect, Chinese-American students in San Francisco not be unlawfully discriminated against because of the failure of schools to teach in their native language. There are similar cases in other parts of the country.

Emerging from these cases are concepts such as "access" which apply as well to the physically handicapped dealing with problems of architectural barriers. Access to education, "suitability" of education, adequate education, appropriate education, are all topics which are raised in one form or another by recent legal developments.

"Accountability" is another emerging concept. We suggest accountability of the system—accountability of the school system and accountability of individuals in the school system. It involves the doctrines of labeling, stigma, unjust classifications of children, and the need to fund special education at a higher level. Funding special education at lower levels than general education is contrary to the Constitution and is a violation of law.

Limitations on the size and capacity of special-education classes violate the Constitution and state law. A denial of rights for homebound and institutionalized training violates state and Federal law in the decision of our courts.

Involuntary labor in public institutions where the labor

is not for therapy is a form of involuntary servitude that may be in violation of the Thirteenth Amendment to the United States Constitution. There may be cruel and unusual punishment violative of the Eighth Amendment of the United States Constitution in some of the conduct of our educational system.

On the periphery, but marching forward also, are the right to procreate and the right to avoid involuntary sterilization. What is voluntary sterilization for the mentally retarded? Voluntary sterilization may be thought to imply that the person has the capacity to give his or her consent, that there is knowledge of the consequences, and that this consent is freely given under circumstances where the alternatives are clear. We don't even have the medical or scientific data to establish that the capacity to make a reasonable choice is available.

The right to mobility for the visually handicapped is another issue. The right to move about freely without obstruction; the right to travel, not only locally through buildings and streets using ramps and having adequate structural facilities, but also on airlines, buses, and trains are all important. Do visually handicapped persons have the right of access to these vehicles and to use them with comfort?

Of value in this area is the case of *Welsch* v. *Likens* and, in the area of involuntary sterilization, the case of *Cox* v. *Stanton.* In general, in the area of accountability, see an article by Professor Trumbull in the March, 1975 issue of *Exceptional Children,* a very short article that sets forth the main cases and projects the direction accountability is likely to take.

The subject of behavior modification is not excepted from legal consideration. To whatever extent chemotherapy and electroshock treatment may be called behavior modification (and I do not so categorize them), they clearly are coming under the courts' control and have been banned under many circumstances. The informed-consent doctrine is applicable. But how about the token system in institutions? Individuals must conform their conduct to win those benefits that the courts now consider to be basic fundamental constitutional rights: the right to food, the right to bedding, the right to clothing, and the right to recreation. This area deserves and is getting considerable attention.

Finally, funding is the important subject involved in two cases, *Serrano* v. *Priest* and *Rodriguez* v. *Texas,* both of which have gone to the United States Supreme Court. Where does the money come from? What about discrimination between school districts based upon the property taxes in each district? Remember, Judge Johnson said, money, or the lack of it, cannot be an excuse for failure to provide adequate treatment.

In California, we not only have a case filed in Sacramento under the impact of the Mills and the PARC decisions, we also have a Master Plan. The Master Plan is a legislative effort to avoid the implications of those decisions and to anticipate them. The Master Plan may exemplify the pioneer role that California special educators have played in keeping this state generally in advance of most other states in the union. But what of the Master Plan? Several outstanding articles dealing with mainstreaming experiences in Washington, D.C., and Pennsylvania have been written. Essentially, the significance of the experience in Washington and Pennsylvania is that there is reluctance to move at all, that there is a tendency to move slowly and cautiously, and that mainstreaming will be a long, drawn-out process. It is essential that the courts be involved to test specific fact situations. But more important to special educators, I think, is that special educators, lawyers, physicians, and all other persons concerned with special education pick up the challenge flung down by the cases and the beginnings of the Master Plan to begin to develop a just and fair and appropriate educational system. See an article called "Schools as Sorters," the work of a young legal writer named David Kirp, in *University of Pennsylvania Law Review* 82. See also his article in *California Law Review* 62, which is most significant.

I earlier referred to the article by Professor Trumbull. I want to paraphrase a portion of that as follows: "Hence, statutes and practices that permit exclusion have been held unconstitutional, zero-reject policies have been established, the implementation of mandatory education for the handicapped has been judicially supervised, compensatory educational opportunities for the handicapped have been ordered, alternatives to in-classroom education have been decreed, school budgets have been ordered to be increased or extended to provide for education for the handicapped, classification criteria have been ordered to be revised, IQ tests have been enjoined, and finally procedural due process has imposed on school exclusion and classification decisions."

Lawyers have limits. More are joining the ranks, but there are too few. The courts have limits. They can decide the large, dramatic cases, but then the day-to-day implementation of these cases rests with educators to make sure that, on a local level, the significance of these decisions becomes immediately clear. Legislators have limits because they engage in the political arena and are subject to political pressures all around them and because they don't have any clear-cut consensus about education in general or about special education.

I opt, in addition, for our role as monitors in lobbying, protesting, and advocating as individuals and organizations of parents, teachers, health professionals, and administrators. We must educate, persuade, negotiate, mediate, arbitrate, and, only as a last resort, litigate. We need patience. We need determined hard work. We need research. Research and more research! I heard Bob Bradfield say this at the 1974 CEC convention at the Sheraton Palace. We need determined hard work, accompanied by what I like to call a kind of controlled rage that the situation is not better.

Finally, special education has an opportunity to teach general education what education ought to be all about. Let us take up the challenge, armed with the decisions that have been wrested from the courts. We are beginning to get to the point where we can devine general education realistically, so that it has meaning within our society beyond the three Rs.

CHAPTER 2

What Research Tells Us about Mainstreaming

Barbara K. Keogh

Although mainstreaming is clearly mandated, we have few data and limited information that provide systematic and clear direction as to effective ways to implement mainstreaming. We have little evidence that delineates program effects. It has been said that academicians labor to state the obvious, but it seems likely that what I am about to do will obscure the obvious. The legal, moral, and ethical imperatives in mainstreaming are obvious. There is, however, considerable obscuring when it comes to the operation, implementation, and evaluation of the mainstreaming effort. Mr. Bancroft comments that lawyers and courts have limitations; I would emphasize that educators, too, have limitations and that we may be rapidly approaching a confrontation of limitations.

It is important that we put both research and programmatic efforts into the frame of reference of the political, social, and legal background that have brought about mainstreaming.[1] While it is possible and likely that the inadequacies and inequities of traditional self-contained and segregated special education programs have been known to educators for many years, it was legal decisions that brought about rapid and sometimes precipitous changes in special-education practices. Despite the unique aspects of many of the cases considered by the courts across the country, there have been a number of common issues and complaints that need delineation. Ross, DeYoung, and Cohen[2] note that there have been arguments as to the inappropriate selection of tests and issues regarding incompetence in the administration of tests, lack of parental involvement in screening and placement decisions, the inadequacy of special-education programs, and the stigmatizing effects of placement procedures and labeling. The effect of all these, of course, has been that traditional selection and placement practices have worked against pupils from ethnic minority and disadvantaged economic backgrounds. In California these inequities were recognized, leading to a series of legal mandates for reform. The California legislature has adopted legislation in two major areas providing background for mainstreaming or transition programs.

Legislation enacted in 1970 dealt essentially with practices in identification, selection, and placement of children in special programs. The second part of that legislation had to do with supplementary education, that is, the so-called transition programs for pupils returning to regular programs. Assembly Bill 1625, entered into the California Statutes as Chapter 1543 of the Education Code, was concerned particularly with the use of intelligence tests in determining elegibility for admission to programs for educable mentally retarded (EMR). This chapter also stipulated that all minors then enrolled in special-education programs for the mentally retarded be re-evaluated before the end of the 1970 calendar year to determine the appropriateness of their placement in those programs. In 1971 Senate Bill 33 stated that children of all ethnic, socioeconomic, and cultural backgrounds be placed in regular classrooms where possible, a directive aimed at a "least restrictive placement" goal. Senate Bill 33 was also concerned with questions of proportional representation of socioeconomic and ethnic groups in classes for the mentally retarded. Specified policies and procedures in identification and placement of pupils added further safeguards to prevent improper placement of minors in programs for the retarded. This bill also required that school districts report to the State Department of Education the proportion of ethnic minorities in classes for EMR. Such reports were to include an explanation of any variance of

15 percent or greater of minority representation in special classes for the mentally retarded when compared with the district population as a whole. The point to be made is that legal pressures and legislative changes which came to bear on special education programs clearly identified some of the directions necessary for program operation.

As a result of legislative action in 1970 and again in 1971, somewhere between 14,000 and 22,000 California pupils were reclassified from EMR status and returned to regular educational placment. Current incidence figures for EMR placements during this period reflect, at least in part, the new and more rigorous requirements for placement. The point is that, by legislative action, these pupils were changed from exceptional to regular status, and were returned to regular programs under varying conditions of support. One might argue that we have found the cure for retardation. It is, of course, difficult, on the basis of incidence figures alone, to determine whether the enrollment drops in EMR programs since 1970 reflect changes brought about by the courts and legislature for reclassification, whether there are fewer pupils begin classified EMR to begin with, whether older EMR pupils have grown up and gotten out of the system, or whether pupils have merely been reclassified into another special education category. In any event, the number of EMR pupils in the state has been reduced dramatically. We need to analyze these findings to determine what, indeed, did happen.

As part of the legislation that required more careful assessment and identification of pupils, the state legislature also provided funds for supplemental or transition programs. In April 1971, the State Department of Education described six possible models for transition programs: resource learning center, consulting teacher, ancillary teacher assistant, in-service training programs, pupil personnel consultants, and bilingual consultants.[3] Variations of these models were also supportable, leading to a diversity of methods of implementation of the transition legislation. Such diversity speaks well for individual responsibility and ingenuity at the district level, but makes systematic program review and monitoring difficult. The guidelines from the Department of Education tended to be general and to deal with the intent of the legislation rather than to provide directions for program specifics. It should be remembered, too, that transition programs were not optional. Reevaluation and reclassification were not. The transition programs were initially viewed as two-year interim programs, though subsequent legislation provided another two years of funding (1972-1974). Despite the temporary nature of the transition funding, almost two hundred and fifty school districts in the state developed formally approved programs. It is likely, of course, that this number represents only a proportion of the number of districts which actually placed former EMR-labeled pupils into regular programs. However, these approximately two hundred and fifty programs, approved by the State Department of Education for special funding, reclassified and reprogramed thousands of pupils. In a sense this sample of districts provided a kind of mini-educational experiment, allowing us a look at mainstreaming practices and problems. Although a *fait accompli*, it is to be hoped that the transition experience in this state will provide guidelines for future, more encompassing mainstream efforts.

A major question facing us is what is the most efficient and effective way of integrating exceptional pupils to the benefit of both these pupils and the regular pupils in the program. It should be emphasized that mere placement in a regular program does not necessarily assure pupil success. In the way of background, let me describe some earlier work done at UCLA in which we looked at a large number of programs for EMR and educationally handicapped (EH) youngsters throughout the state.[4] We found that EMR pupils on the average had been in EMR programs for over four years and that they were about three years behind grade level in arithmetic, spelling, and reading. The point to be made is that, when transition pupils were reclassified and put back into the regular programs, many returned with severe academic disadvantage. They were already significantly behind their regular-class peers, and the regular-class program was not necessarily structured to meet effectively the particular needs of these children. Preliminary findings from current work at UCLA[5] and from the comprehensive study of Myers, MacMillan, and Yoshita[6] suggest that the transition pupil's academic disadvantage continues despite his placement in regular programs. Overall the national findings, along with the California data, are discouraging in regard to the academic competence of the youngsters who are reclassified and moved into the mainstream.

Despite the somewhat discouraging data regarding academic achievement, there is evidence from a number of studies that allows a more optimistic view of the integration of pupils in terms of social adjustment. Gampel, Gottlib, and Harrison, for example, have found that there is a positive effect of adequate peer models on mainstreamed pupils, and that the regular-classroom environment does indeed affect the behavior of former EMR pupils.[7] My colleagues at Berkeley, Gilbert Guerin and Kathleen Szatlocky, have also found that EMR pupils integrated into regular classes were not identifiable from normal achieving children as far as classroom behavior was concerned.[8] This finding has been supported by others, including the work in Texas under "Project Prime."[9] There is thus some research evidence to suggest that mainstreaming has positive social and behavioral effects on youngsters formerly in self-contained programs. The issue is more cloudy and less optimistic where academic skill achievement is concerned.

As part of an effort to clarify some of the mainstream/ integration questions, we took on the task of looking *post hoc* at transition programs in approximately two hundred and fifty districts in California.[10] This project was carried out in cooperation with the Department of Education under the UCLA-CSULA Special Education Research Program. We were interested in finding out the programatic modifications school districts made to implement transition legislation. In particular, we wanted to know: (a) What kinds of procedures and methods were used to identify and re-evaluate pupils for eligibility for programs? (b) What kinds of staff development were employed? (c) How did districts evaluate the effectiveness of their programs? (d) What did district personnel identify as problems, and (e) How did they think future programs might be handled more efficiently?

In the first phase of the project, we interviewed administrators in ten school districts, getting an in-depth picture of what things worked and what didn't. On the basis of that information, we developed a questionnaire that was sent to all other formally approved transition districts within the state. About 73 percent of these districts responded. The findings I report are based on input from over one hundred and sixty districts.

Let me summarize the major findings of this project. First, all districts in our sample did indeed meet the state laws and legislative requests by reviewing pupils who were in EMR programs. The nature of that review differed dramatically, however. In some districts, old school records by which the child originally had been placed in EMR status were reviewed. If the child had an IQ of above 70, he was automatically removed and placed in a transition program or in a regular class. Other districts retested all ethnic minority pupils in the programs. Still others retested all pupils in the EMR program. Districts used a variety of defining criteria but, it should be emphasized, the major reason for return to the regular program was psychometric scores. That is interesting because, despite recognition of the problems of psychometric tests when applied to ethnic minority pupils[11] and despite the long legal history over possible inequities in psychometrics when used with ethnic minoirities,[12] it was still psychometric scores that had the heaviest weight in determining pupils' eligibility for regular-class placement.

Second, ethnic characteristics of the pupils reclassified and placed in transition programs tended to reflect the ethnic characteristics of the district. That is, high Anglo districts reclassified high numbers of Anglo pupils, high black districts reclassifed high numbers of black pupils, and so forth. However, it should be emphasized that many districts with high proportions of ethnic minority pupils apparently made especially vigorous efforts to utilize transition programs. According to the administrators' reports, estimates of numbers of ethnic minority pupils reclassified in those districts often exceeded the proportion of ethnic minoirities in the school population. Because Anglos are the majority group in California public schools, by actual count more Anglo pupils were reclassified and placed in the transition programs. However, the numbers of Spanish-surname and black pupils reclassifed and placed in transitional status exceeded their proportional representation in the districts. In this sense, California districts were apparently making a direct response to the legislation.

Third, a variety of transition options were used. Remember that the Department of Education recommended six possible fundable plans, but districts developed diverse and different programs of implementation. Some districts reclassified all eligible pupils from EMR to EH status, a solution with little direct influence on regular education. Other districts placed all former EMR pupils in full-day self-contained transition programs. In a sense such procedures may create a new special-education category: Transition. Other districts placed all former EMR pupils in full-day programs and used resource models, paraprofessional aides, or the like. The single most popular administrative model was regular-class placement with paraprofessional aides. The majority of transition options utilized some kind of tutorial arrangement in an effort to provide individualized help to pupils in subject-matter areas. Almost none of the districts used the learning-disability grouping plan, the option we had anticipated would be a high-priority choice.

Because most of the children went into full-day regular programs with some individualized help provided in that setting, it is obvious that staff development is a critical aspect of integration efforts. Of the total number of districts studied, only half had in-service training directly related to transition programs. This was the case despite our finding that most of the pupils were in regular full-day classes, dealt with by a regular-education-trained teacher, by school psychologists, and by principals whose primary concerns had not been with special education. It is interesting, too, that where in-service training was provided it was directed almost exclusively at direct instructional personnel, that is, teachers and teacher-aides. Few districts provided staff development for principals, school psychologists, guidance workers, school nurses, or others working with transition pupils and with those who teach them. For the most part, the effectiveness of the in-service programing is unknown, except that administrators expressed concern that they needed help in planning more adequate in-service training. In general, administrators' subjective comments reflected a need for more detailed and comprehensive in-service training for both teaching and administrative personnel. We interpreted those comments to suggest that in-service training was not entirely satisfactory in meeting the needs of the receiving teachers and did not touch upon the changed role of school psychologists or administrators who are involved with mainstreaming efforts. Although the preparation of members of the regular school staff for working effectively with transition pupils was viewed as an important part of the transition or mainstreaming effort, districts, for the most part, provided minimal or cursory efforts in this regard. There is considerable evidence that the results were, in general, unsatisfactory. This is not to say that there were not good programs in some districts. In general, however, the critical importance of staff development was not recognized.

In terms of program effects or outcomes, administrators' reports were generally positive, but many indicated that they had mixed views of transition programs for both pupils and school personnel. There was agreement that the review and reclassification process had corrected a number of inequities in EMR labeling and placement. There was less confidence that transition programing *per se* had been consistently beneficial to transition or regular-class pupils. Placement in regular-class programs was viewed as having positive effects on pupils' social adjustment, self-concept, and the like. There was agreement that transition placement, as opposed to EMR placement, had removed the stigma of the EMR label. However, there was real concern as to whether there was academic benefit from the regular placement and whether the programs were adequate to provide for the individual needs of pupils. There was also considerable agreement that transition placement had worked a hardship on regular classroom teachers and that many of these teachers were neither prepared nor enthusiastic about serving former EMR pupils.

The high degree of uncertainty about program effects was due, in large part, to inadequate systems for monitoring, evaluation, and systematic collection of data. As a personal aside, I can say that after having spent the last four and a half years working with school districts on a variety of research projects, I must conclude that school personnel in general are very poor record-keepers. Often, at the end of a particular program, we don't know what's happened, under what circumstances, or to whom. This is certainly true in the case of the transition programs. At the end of the four-year period, it is not possible to determine with any degree of confidence what were the significant program parameters or outcomes. Subjectively, the perceptions of the administrators were positive, but few districts planned to continue transition efforts after the state funding ended. It is clear that the efforts that led to reclassification and removal of the pejorative label were successful. Approximately 20,000 pupils were reclassified. Outcomes at the next level, the effectiveness of educational programing, are cloudy. Data on which to evaluate program effects on transition and regular pupils are not available. Comprehensive descriptions of operational aspects of programs are limited. In a sense, we are left with unknown procedures and unknown outcomes. The point becomes critical when we consider the strong national support for mainstreaming exceptional children in regular school programs and the newly developed Master Plan in this state.

The transition program in California, although no longer formally operational, may well serve as an indication of what is to come. On the basis of our findings, we would like to make several recommendations to be considered by districts implementing mainstreaming efforts. We view as the number one priority the preparation of regular-school personnel to deal effectively with exceptional children. Preparation must be included at both preservice and in-service training levels and must involve the full range of professionals and paraprofessionals serving exceptional children. Most in-service training has been directed at instructional personnel only; in our opinion, it is often not adequate. When we view the range of services required for successful integration or mainstreaming of exceptional youngsters, it is clear that we must involve the full gamut of school professionals, including school superintendents. As an interesting aside, one of the recommendations made in follow-up work by a UCLA postdoctoral fellow[13] was that, when new programs are to be implemented on a statewide basis, the first level of in-service training should be conducted by the Department of Education and should be directed specifically at superintendents of schools. Boyd's argument, of course, is that if a program is to be successful the person at the top must know what it's all about and must support it. In any case, continuing training is a critical aspect of program change.

A second recommendation has to do with consideration of a variety of options within the regular programs which will ensure the appropriateness of educational programing for particular children or groups of children. The state has proposed six program models. From our data, none has been overwhelming in its success. At the same time, none has been shown to be ineffective. The point is that few districts have proposed consistent and comprehensive program modifications that ensure the adequacy of services to exceptional children mainstreamed in the regular program. It is possible that some of the program options utilized may actually impede successful teaching and successful learning within the regular program. It is critical that we match the programs positively to the characteristics of the children. The problem is not simple. As an example, children with severe hearing impairment may be integrated in regular programs if communication is possible. For children with speech-reading or other language skills, mainstreaming requires only relatively minor program modifications. If the child does not speech-read, however, it is necessary that there be some kind of alternative language available for communication to occur. The question is not "Should deaf children be integrated?" but rather "How can deaf children be integrated? What program accommodations are necessary to ensure the success of that integration?" We argue for more differentiated program accommodations to maximize successful integration. The six program models already described are mostly administrative and mainly provide a place to start.

Finally, we argue strongly for the development of comprehensive, feasible, and usable systems of data collection relative to program outcomes. This quite clearly involves recognition and acceptance of the value of differing outcomes (viz., social adjustment and/or academic achievement) and argues for the necessity of careful monitoring of the progress of children and programs. I reiterate: School personnel are poor record-keepers, and as a consequence we often can't tell what, indeed, has happened.

In conclusion, I wish to reemphasize the importance of the mainstream effort for all pupils and their teachers. At the same time, I make the cautionary statement that the state of the art may not be sufficiently developed for us to be fully confident of the ways we are going to accomplish the critical legal and legislative mandates. I am concerned at the possible negative effects of mainstreaming for some children, and argue that "due process" must also protect the child from being placed in situations in which he will be hurt. Mere enthusiasm is not enough. We are at a time when we need major and systematic research and evaluation efforts directed at determination of programs relative to pupil needs. The "transition experience" in California may well be an important step in understanding mainstreaming. It is to be hoped that we will learn from this bit of immediate history. On the basis of our review of these programs, two questions have high priority: How can we serve pupils with a broad range of abilities, talents, skills, and experiences in the regular school program? How do we know what we have accomplished?

NOTES

1. D. L. Kirp, "Schools as Sorters: The Constitutional and Policy Implications of Student Classification," *University of Pennsylvania Law Review* 121: 4 (1973); F. J. Weintraub, "Recent Influences and Law Regarding the Identification and Educational Placement of Children," *Focus on Exceptional Children* 4: 2 (1972).

2. S. Ross, H. DeYoung, and J. S. Cohen, "Confrontation: Special Education and the Law," *Exceptional Children* 4:7 (1971): 5-12.

3. E. Gonzales and L. Brinegar, "Transition Programs Authorized by Education Code Section 18102, 11. Communication to County and District Superintendents of Schools." (Sacramento: Division of Special Education and Division of Instruction, April 1971).

4. B. K. Keogh, L. D. Becker, M. B. Kukic, and S. J. Kukic, *Programs for Educationally Handicapped and Educable Mentally Retarded Pupils: Review and Recommendations* (technical report, SERP 1972 A-11; University of California, Los Angeles, 1972).

5. B. K. Keogh and M. L. Levitt, "Special Education in the Mainstream: A Confrontation of Limitations?" *Focus on Exceptional Children* 8:1 (1976): 1-11; M. L. Levitt, B. K. Keogh, and R. J. Hall, *Follow-Up Study of Transition Pupils in Regular Education Programs* (technical report, SERP 1975 A-11. University of California, Los Angeles, 1975).

6. C. E. Myers, D. L. MacMillan, and R. Yoshita, *Correlates of Success in Transition EMR's; Final Report* (Bureau of Education for the Handicapped, U. S. Office of Education, 1975).

7. D. H. Gampel, J. Gottlib, and R. H. Harrison, "Comparison of Classroom Behavior of Special-Class EMR, Integrated EMR, Low IQ, and Non-Retarded Children," *American Journal of Mental Deficiency* 79:1 (1974): 16-21.

8. G. R. Guerin and K. Szatlocky, "Integration Programs for the Mildly Retarded" (paper presented at the annual meeting of the California Association of School Psychologists, San Diego, March 1974).
9. Texas Education Agency, Department of Special Education and Special Schools, *Impact of Intramural Research Program: Project Prime in Texas* (a report to the Commission of Education, U. S. Office of Education, September 1974).
10. B. K. Keogh, M. L. Levitt, G. Robson, and K. S. Chan, *A Review of Transition Programs in California Public Schools* (technical report; SERP 1974 A-2. University of California, Los Angeles, 1974).
11. J. R. Mercer, "Sociological Perspectives on Mild Retardation," in H. C. Haywood (ed.), *Social-Cultural Aspects of Mental Retardation* (New York: Appleton-Century-Crofts, 1970).
12. D. L. Kirp, W. Buss, and P. Kuriloff, "Legal Reform of Special Education: Empirical Studies and Procedural Proposals," *California Law Review* 62:1 (1974): 40-155.
13. R. M. Boyd, *School Administrators' Views of Inservice Training for Transition Program Personnel* (technical report, SERP 1975 A-1; University of California, Los Angeles, 1975).

REFERENCE

Keogh, B. K. Levitt, M. L., and Robson, G. *Historical and Legislative Antecedents of Decertification and Transition Programs in California Public Schools.* Technical report, SERP 1974 A-3. University of California, Los Angeles, 1974.

CHAPTER 3

Mainstreaming:

Historical Perspectives

Maynard Reynolds

The most conspicuous trend in the field of special education, and perhaps in all of education today, is mainstreaming. Mainstreaming is more than a way of providing special education to handicapped children in the schools. It is part of a general movement throughout the country to end the isolation and neglect of handicapped persons. The movement has been growing over the past two decades and is affecting every institution in our society, not just the schools. Fundamentally, it is a reflection of the democratic philosophy that equal access to societal institutions and resources is the right of all individuals, however different from the majority they may be.

Mainstreaming has been stimulated by many factors in and out of the schools. Judicial pronouncements are stressing the rights of individuals, sometimes as distinguished from the rights or convenience of institutions. Residential institutions that isolate individuals from normal community life have become suspect. Indeed, the placement of exceptional persons in set-aside residential arrangements has been slowed; and the populations of isolating institutions are emptying back into the community. Schools are developing local programs for severely handicapped children as part of their obligation to the community. In addition, schools are developing new administrative formats to serve children with mild and moderate handicaps through such means as resource rooms, consulting-teacher arrangements, and the like. The boundary lines between regular education and special education are eroding. Specialists are learning to serve clients indirectly through teaming arrangements with regular teachers, for example rather than just through direct services. Greater use is being made of instructional management systems in regular education to permit careful and sensitive attention to individual pupils. The use of norm-reference testing, social comparison testing, is being phased down; and, instead, there is a sharp upturn in individually oriented testing and monitoring systems not involving social comparisons.

Such events as these, and they are only a few, connect with each other meaningfully. As a whole, they represent a strong general movement to spread educational opportunities to all individuals. Possibly economists would tell us that we've only lately become affluent enough to consider public policy that spreads hope to all members of our society. This new trend stresses inclusiveness rather than isolation, even to the point of serving individuals with extraordinarily exceptional needs in the natural environment of the community whenever feasible rather than sending them off to special stations. Perhaps much of this trend could be summarized under the heading of "individualism." In operational terms, it seems reasonable to use the term "mainstreaming" as well.

Mainstreaming is sometimes presented as a crude and cruel tossing of handicapped youngsters from special-class boxes back to regular-class boxes. It is a cruel crudity when it is nothing more than that, and it should be opposed by special educators. But mainstreaming can be something much better than that. What I mean by mainstreaming is a whole set of dispositions or attitudes and operations through which exceptional children are served in their natural homes and schools through the community environment and by means of which the displacement of children to isolation is reduced. In a sense, it represents a reversal of that whole negative cascade in which we have, for too long, first rejected some children from regular classes, placed them in special stations in the school, and then moved them to the end of the line: those residential institutions where there is so little of human freedom.

What I would like to do is to explore what might be some of the sources of this broad trend I refer to as mainstreaming. I will have to sketch its history very rapidly. I think it is reasonable to view the history of systematic efforts to provide education for exceptional children as falling into four periods. The first is the residential school period. In the nineteenth century, as most people know, we established residential schools patterned on the model of the asylum in Europe. Residential centers for limited numbers of youngsters were set aside.

Then, at about the turn of the century, we entered what I would call the community prototype period. Superintendents of some of the larger city school districts visited the residential schools, saw programs of interest, and sought to establish similar facilities. Slowly, through most of the first half of this century, we developed special classes and special schools. At first, teachers went to places like Vineland to obtain their training. The curriculum, emerging from institutions like Vineland and Gallaudet College, developed relatively slowly.

The third period, what I call the period of explosion of a simple model, spans about twenty-five years, from 1945 to 1970. As if to make up for the neglect of centuries in one very large effort, a remarkable surge of activity on behalf of handicapped children began shortly after World War II. Our largest states launched programs on a broad scale to serve handicapped children in local schools. Numerous colleges and universities organized programs to train teachers for special education. California was one of the large states that launched a program in the 1940s. The very distinguished training program at San Francisco State University, then known as San Francisco State College, under the leadership of Leo Cain, was formed in that period. Read back in the *Exceptional Children*'s journals in the late forties and you'll find the story of that time. Another of the quite remarkable developments, at about the same time, was in Illinois, where the large program at the University of Illinois was launched. Before that time, there was relatively little teacher-training at the universities. There was some teacher-training at Teachers College, some that Sam Kirk and others were associated with at Milwaukee, and some at Ypsilanti. The movement in California and in Illinois really came in conjunction with large efforts by the public schools in some of our states.

Between 1945 and 1970, the number of children served in special stations in the public schools increased about 700 percent. The number of colleges and universities involved in special education increased correspondingly. It was in that period that the parents of handicapped children organized and became a potent force, mainly through political action. In 1950, the National Association for Retarded Children was formed in my home city of Minneapolis. I recall very well the vigorous action of that group. In 1952, during my first year at the University of Minnesota, we called a meeting of all parent groups we knew about in Minneapolis and St. Paul. Thirty-five groups came to the meeting and, out of this meeting, we formed a very aggressive federation called the Minnesota Council of Special Education.

It was also in that period that the nation was attempting to deal very sensitively with young men who had been injured in World War II and the Korean conflict. Rehabilitation facilities in veterans hospitals were enlarged, and new research programs to further rehabilitation were established in various institutions and agencies. Colleges and universities expanded departments in clinical psychology, speech pathology, and physical medicine. The influences of investigations on behalf of veterans spread to the research and training being carried on for exceptional children. In those days, when I first met Georgie Lee Abel, she and Kay Gruber were working with the American Federation for the Blind. They were instrumental in forming specialized programs on behalf of blinded veterans, particularly the Hines Center in Illinois. Georgie Lee Abel helped build the connection between that program and the schools. At San Francisco State, in the peripatology program, you have a staff that has organic connections back to that veterans hospitals movement.

It should be noted that, in this rapid increase in programing, in the sheer quantitative leap, there were really few technological or ideological advances. There were some innovations, such as the development of low-vision aids and individual electronic hearing aids, but they are of limited significance in understanding the truly massive changes of the period. In the main, that period of very rapid development can be said to have been based on simple models of the past. This is not to imply that the two-and-a-half-decade period was totally barren of ideas. On the contrary, some of the trends we see now were generated during those years. One of the things that happened was that programs for a vast array of handicapped children came under one umbrella. At San Francisco State University and at my university, the University of Minnesota, programs for the preparation of teachers of the deaf, teachers of the blind, and teachers of retarded and cerebral-palsied children came under one leadership. We began working together as a department. We had organic ties back to highly categorical and isolated institutions for the deaf, the retarded, and the blind, and crippled; but we were now "living in one tent." Similarly, very large programs were developing in the public schools with administrators being employed to oversee broad programs. I think we began to see that the categories we had been dealing with were really not, as one of my friends said, "carvings of nature at its joints." They weren't all that real. They were to a considerable extent very human constructions. In this context, there developed a kind of remarkable noncategorical program that in many places emerged under the rubric of "learning disabilities." In California, the program was called "Educationally Handicapped." We found children "falling through the cracks," and programs began to emerge that were not for the traditional kind of categorical handicap. Nevertheless, the inclusion of these new areas in special education was welcomed, at least as a transitional step toward something that we should seek for the future.

The fourth period began in about 1970. I would call this the period of negotiations, negotiations for more integration. As a result of the experience gained from the very busy period of 1945-1970, the field of special education began negotiating in the early seventies for more integrated placement of exceptional children in the public schools and communities. The changes were quite fundamental.

But to complete the brief historical statement before examining those recent changes more closely, let me summarize by calling your attention to the fact that the whole history of special education, the systematic attempt to educate exceptional children, can be viewed in terms of one steady trend described by the term "progressive inclusion." Handicapped children have emerged from total neglect, first into isolated residential schools for just a few, then into isolated community settings, mostly special classes and special schools, and lately into much more integrated arrangements. In the long view, the current mainstreaming trend, I think, is not preperly viewed as a minor pendulum swing or a temporary enthusiasm. It is part of a steady, progressive inclusive trend, one that I believe testifies to a kind of moral development in our society. It is also one I would unashamedly claim for the field of special education if we but open ourselves to the challenge. Admittedly, mainstreaming is somewhat controversial, as the very title of this book indicates. But it seems to me it's upon us, and the movement is much broader than just special education. The forces are much broader than those controlled by special educators. Mr. Bancroft states that literally hundreds of legal cases are providing force to the movement. The trends in the field of mental health, criminology, and social welfare are in much the same direction. The movement is so general that, to some extent, the controversies we discuss in special education become almost academic.

Let me turn now to an examination of some of the forces that seem to be operating, particularly since 1970. The first is the transition on the part of the parent groups from political action to a court-oriented approach to securing services for their children. The concepts of right to education, least restrictive environment, and due process are emerging. The judicial imperative to educators has derived from that new strategy on the part of parent groups. I do say "parent groups" because, in my belief, the wave of court cases throughout the country has been carefully orchestrated, in the main, by people associated with parent groups.

Second are special problems in connection with minority groups. During that busy period of 1945 to 1970, action was initiated by parent groups concerned with the various exceptionality categories. Those groups drew their membership and active participants from parents, in the main, of quite severely handicapped children. A high proportion of the membership of those organizations is white, middle-class, and relatively affluent. However, as you know, the programs they instigated affected a great many children other than their own. In fact, the greatest impact of these groups was felt in the urban ghetto by minority-group children, especially in programs for the educable mentally retarded and emotionally disturbed, categories that carry the most stigma. The President's Committee on Mental Retardation reported in 1968 that children from impoverished and minority-group homes were fifteen times more likely to be diagnosed mentally retarded as were children from higher-income families. The report also indicated that three fourths of the nation's diagnosed mentally retarded children are to be found in the isolated, impoverished urban and rural slums. As awareness grew of what was happening in schools and minority communities, resentment and resistance were aroused. As a result, the administrators of school systems in the larger cities have been given a virtual mandate to reverse the expansion of special-education programs and to eliminate the testing, categorizing, and labeling practices that are associated with placement in those programs. In his review of Michael Young's book *Rise of Meritocracy*, David Reisman lauded this type of resistance of parents, as he put it, to having their children "fall like brass in Plato's social system." The conflicting interests of categorical parent groups and minority groups obviously requires accommodation. The forces for such accommodation are especially strong in the larger cities, where administrators are under that virtual mandate not to move past testing, labeling, and grouping practices. Civil rights officers at the United States Department of Health, Education, and Welfare have added their force to change patterns in special education. Charles Meisgeier will tell you that Houston was one of those cities impacted by civil rights officers who observed that the proportion of black and Chicano children in special-education programs was much too high. The school district was directed to find a new format through which children needing intensive services could receive them without negative labeling. That same mandate is occurring in other cities. Note that there's no resistance, I think, to the provision of intensive educational services to children of minority-group parents. But there is resistance to the system of special education that starts with labels and stigma. It is because of this new formats are emerging for special education, such as

45

resource rooms, diagnostic-prescriptive centers, and consulting-teacher models. All these formats involve teamwork by both regular and special educators. But the problems of implementing new models of special service to the satisfaction of all elements of the community are difficult. Unfortunately, much of our state legislation, and some proposed Federal legislation, still requires or would require crude categories and negative labels as starting points for special education. I have had very great concern about recent Federal legislation that would have required national uniform categories of children, would have promised a lot of money, but on the head of each child. It would have been the largest bounty hunt for children, by category, we've ever seen.

Hopefully this unnecessary practice, excessive labeling, will be overcome. I've mentioned the litigious action of parent groups and the conflict between the interests of minority-group parents and traditional categorical parent groups.

The developments and changes in measurement systems or technology are another very important factor. Here too there is no space to discuss the subject in detail. I think very often of the task that Binet apparently faced in Paris at the beginning of the century. He was asked to develop a means for predicting the academic achievement of youngsters. He succeeded remarkably well, at least compared with the general validity of most psychological predictions. The ideas of prediction and capacity quickly became linked. Predictions of academic progress based on Binet tests were regularly interpreted, within a short time, as measurements of pupils' capacities to complete a school program. This linkage of simple prediction and capacity was taken for granted for perhaps a half a century. Almost as much energy has gone into the prediction of academic achievement as into the prediction of horse races or the stock market. For academic prediction, general intelligence test results have been by far the most commonly used device. An early side-effect of the movement was development of individualized reading systems that became a matter of misguided fairness, a belief that some children should be expected to achieve more and some less and that report cards should reflect each child's achievement in relation to his individual capacity.

I have always felt that, if we knew enough to predict perfectly every child's achievement, every child would be achieving exactly as expected. Only our imperfection in prediction has yielded these strange notions of capacity.

A refinement of this procedure was the special attention given children whose capacity was high but achievement low, the so-called under-achievers or learning disabled. It might have been argued equally well that all children were doing exactly as should be expected if only we knew enough to make accurate predictions. In any event, the discrepancy cases could easily have been called the over-predicted rather than the under-achievers, placing the blame on the predictors rather than on the child. The discrepancies between mental age and achievement are not necessarily indicators of special need for clinical services. I struggled with that for years when I worked at the Psychoeducational Center at the University of Minnesota. Mostly, what we succeeded in doing was confusing students, I think. But millions of dollars have been invested in supporting this curious assumption. Strangely, these discrepancy variables, reflecting differences between "capacity" and "achievement," have never been carefully studied. Yet they have become enormously popular in drawing distinctions between remedial or learning-disability cases and the retarded. The assumption was that children with high capacity but low achievement belong to a different category than those showing uniformly low, flat profiles. There was a case made for pervasive pessimism about the educability of children with low-capacity estimates. No wonder the parents of EMR children, or children who scored low on these tests, became hostile toward the schools.

A subtle form of discrepancy analysis used profile interpretations involving the assumption that the general level of a profile, such as on a WISC or ITPA, yields some kind of expectancy level, and departures from the flat median line represent needs or potentialities for remediation. By some mystical process, the average of several scores becomes the expected level on each variable. Presumably, flat profiles are nothing more than abstractions over large numbers of children. This form of discrepancy analysis will not stand up to rigorous examination any better than simpler approaches using general intelligence as the standard. One of the reasons we have gotten into difficulty is that we have overused general or broad-band variables. In the main, general intelligence yields prediction in almost any and every setting and yet helps little in choosing. Just as intelligence predicts success in every program that you have at San Francisco State but is of little value to the student in choosing among them, so general intelligence tests predict, for those who score low in a negative way, about almost any program but really do not help in making a choice among them. What we have been party to, I think, is using instruments that have a simple kind of predictive validity for making selection-rejection decisions. However, when a youngster is rejected, that's no indication that he's better off somewhere else. It's simply an indication that the prediction, for him, in the first environment or the given environment is not favorable as compared with others. What the courts are asking of us now is that, when we propose alternative placement, we look at those variables. You must look at the child and you must look at the environment. If you displace the child, it is not because he is predicted not to do well in the regular class, but because you have evidence that he will do better in the very specialized arrangement.

Cronback tells the story of the efforts in England to predict achievement of gifted youngsters through multiple correlation techniques. They pull out youngsters who score very high and send them to special schools, thinking that the variables that yield high prediction in the regular school situation will help identify those who will do still better in the special situation. This has not been the case. I think the notions of Cronback, indicating that we must consider simultaneously the situations, the environmental differences, and the variables that produce interactions, are really fundamental.

B. F. Skinner has argued that we have permitted the adjective, as in "intelligent behavior," to become the noun, "intelligence"; and then we make futile speculations about its determinants. Broad-band tests make predictions about children, but they're not very useful in helping make a difference in the lives of children. That's the problem. Schools are there, not to make grand predictions about youngsters, but to make a difference in their lives. What the teacher does in school must make a difference. The problem is to attend to children and to arrange environments so that we make a constructive difference in the lives of children. I think we've only begun to realize how complex that is.

I must mention, altogether too inadequately here, the development of procedures for measuring behavior techniques, contributed by many specialists. A great many of them in the fields of special education, precision-teaching, and associated measurement technology help us observe children carefully, do experiments, check performance, assess what appears to be developing. The whole move is toward use of domain- and criterion-referenced testing and objective-related testing, and away from norm-based testing. That whole movement has been extremely important in special education and is spreading to all of education.

I believe that there has been a basic philosophical change, too, which is reflected in the court decisions. There was a period in the 1950s when it was seriously argued by special educators that we accept trainable mentally retarded in the school programs simply on the basis of the likelihood of their becoming contributing members of their families or contributing members within their community. Now, very clearly, the argument has turned. It is enhancement of the life of the individual that is the test, and not whether he or she will contribute later to the community. That change, making enhancement of the life of the individual the test rather than value ot an institution or society as a whole, has been most fundamental. I sicken a bit when I attend legislative hearings and occasionally hear people make the case for rehabilitation programs on the basis of the high-employment records of those they have served, with a return of the cost of their programs through income tax. We have surpassed that, and we now offer training programs to teach youngsters to feed themselves simply because it gives them a life with broader options and greater satisfactions, even though the programs are costly. The achievement is of great importance.

We face the development of mainstreaming in the context of very difficult times in education. With decreasing enrollments and teachers losing jobs, it is not a desirable era. We face the mainstreaming imperative with funding systems that, in many states, are out of date, yielding more money when children are in isolated, categorical arrangements than when they are in integrated arrangements. This is going to be a very complex matter to turn around. We will have to be very careful about the issue of ownership and proprietorship as we undertake training activities in support of mainstreaming. The task we face is much more complex than simply offering a three-credit course in special education for all teachers. We must get the social studies teachers to do their own training, the elementary teachers to do their own training, and the superintendents, within their own groups, to give leadership rather than to take lessons from us. That's going to require a very complex and mature kind of arrangement.

We have particular problems in secondary and vocational schools that would seem to require basic reorganization well beyond what we face in elementary schools. We face problems of excess in "process." One of the leading figures in the Boston area told me that the costs of special education in that area may double this year. A lot of that cost goes to formal hearings, to reevaluation, evaluation upon evaluation. In the name of "process" we may get more process than is due. We must avoid letting the cost of mere processing in formal arrangements which are nonproductive in the lives of children become too consuming an aspect of our work.

We face problems of remoteness and disconnectedness as parents are given rights to secure their own diagnosis of their children. A terrible irresponsibility might result from your being told that you must organize a program of maintainance for some physical function when your informants don't have all the budgetary problems that you do. You might find a psychologist, a mental health center, or a hospital telling you exactly what kind of treatment programs in reading you should implement. We get very bad habits when we get that kind of disconnectedness, and I believe a moral imperative as well, to reconstruct our schools so as to be more inclusive of all children—inclusive in the ultimate sense. I believe that we should proceed in this with determination and satisfaction. It is not a reversal but a further step in what has been a long journey in special education. There are problems rooted in our limited knowledge. We don't know how to do all the things we're asked to do. There are limits in lawyers and in the courts as there are in teachers and education. We have problems rooted in matters of inconvenience, difficulties and expense in changing toward a totally inclusive program. Our difficulties lie partly in our tendancy to let institutional goals or institutional convenience dominate. When our knowledge and skill are marginal or when the task is difficult, we tend not to act, to let the program erode. We fall into a select-reject mentality and let some youngsters slip aside.

The problem, for us, is to support all those youngsters who have been or who are likely to be rejected from the natural environment of children. What we want, presumably, is to build stations into our homes, schools, and other aspects of the community that provide support and opportunities for all children. The negative cascade has reversed. Special education has two options. It can repair to its accustomed enclave and attend to only the more severely handicapped. I think a better course, a larger challenge, is to open up our relationships with regular education and try to build unitary school systems that indeed serve all children.

Mr. Bancroft says that the lawyers and the courts have limits and that the challenge flows largely to educators to implement some of the mandates coming from the courts. Dr. Keogh mentions that we may be approaching a confrontation concerning limitations. I think that our limitations can often appear to be unwillingness and that there is the tendency sometimes for legislators and bureaucrats to add layers of rules or regulations or legislation as if the problem were one of simple compliance in these difficult situations. The face is, I think, that very often we do not know adequately how to solve all of the problems. It is all the more important then, I think, that we create systems through which we can share what insights we have and contribute to one another as we try to meet this very significant challenge.

51

CHAPTER 4

Mainstreaming:

Assessment Issues

Asa G. Hilliard

At the University of Denver, I was very fortunate in having an excellent professor who taught logic. I've always wanted to see things clearly, and logic certainly helped. My professor once gave an assignment that utilized nonsense syllables and nonsense words. He used something I still remember from our logic text: "All spathling quidities are things that frobble with froy and so are sladwishey things." From that, of course, you could draw some logical conclusions about things that "frobble with froy" and about "sladwishey things," *even if there were none*! So logic and truth don't always have anything in common. In fact, logic can be completely independent of truth.

I also remember a piece of writing that had great impact on me and my thinking over a number of years. His book, *Language in Thought and Action*, is one of the positive things the people remember about S. I. Hayakawa.

I come to problems using a perspective that was developed by insights such as come from these sources and from the belief that one must keep asking questions about everything. That latter point is very important in education. I don't think we ask basic questions about what we're doing very often. Looking at the area of assessment, I'll try to illustrate that by comparing what I think are proper procedures with what a surgeon does. You can't really help anything, even though you like people, if you don't cut a little bit and go inside. It may look messy while you're in there, but that's the way to see what's wrong. On the other hand, if you leave people open and bleeding, you still haven't helped. I think you have to close up and clean up if you're to approach a cure. I would like to approach our subject in that way.

I've read all four of Carlos Castaneda's books several times. They have helped me to articulate and clarify my perspective on the so-called "real world." Castaneda makes a distinction between "looking" and "seeing." I'd like to make that distinction too, since we, special educators and regular educators, talk about, "look" around, and assess schools and what they do. When you walk through schools, special-education classes are bound to impress you, especially classes for the "retarded" and the "educationally handicapped." If you are any kind of observer at all, you must be impressed with the ethnic make-up of the classes. But few people go beyond that and see other kinds of interesting patterns in those placements. One interesting phenomenon about the placements is that, within ethnic groups, patterns occur. For example, it is the black male rather than the black female who is disproportionately represented in some of these classes for the "retarded" and "educationally handicapped."

If you assume a genetic explanation for "cognitive deficits," then you wind up with a problem on your hands which, apparently, very few people have addressed. Why is there a distinction by sex? We had a similar problem a few years ago in the "difference in IQ between women and men." Every educational psychologist taught that, at first, women had higher IQs than men and then later men caught up and passed the women. That "fact," which many teachers carried around in their heads, was really not a fact at all but an artifact of the way in which we collected the data. The drop-out rate was different for men and women. Men tended to drop out and the IQs of those who remained were naturally higher. So there was a systematic influence on the data that led us to some erroneous conclusions about IQs. We would have seen this clearly if we had gone further than "looking" and had tried to "see" exactly what was happening.

Unfortunately, I think, our response in education very often tends to be a paper data, rather than to real clinical experience. As a result, I think we've very often abandoned our responsibility as clinical observers. Instead of relying upon our senses buttressed by the kinds of instruments and tools that exist, we rely on the tools—or, worse than that, on the evidence that is summarized from the tools—in making judgments about systems. There is a real danger here.

A young friend of mine, Dr. Gregory Ochoa, told me in a conversation, "You know, Asa, I was labeled retarded, and I believed it until I was out of high school; and then someone helped me to see that I wasn't. I was responding to myself as if I were mentally retarded. Later I became a good student—actually an outstanding student." I responded to Greg by indicating that I've been doing an informal survey. It may surprise many to know, if you haven't done a similar survey (again, looking and seeing), that blacks who hold a PhD have a common experience. It crops up again and again in surveys. At some point in their school careers, they were told either that they were mentally retarded or did not have college ability. I am one of those, as a matter of fact, who was told in junior high that I should not think of college but should consider manual arts. Fortunately, I had some teachers who encouraged me to do the opposite. But my point is that there is systematic misassessment in education. I'm not saying that only to be negative. I'm really trying to get a grip on what is real because, if we're going to do anything about the kinds of assessment that we do, we have to take more than a peripheral, superficial look at what goes on in assessment. We must understand the actual instruments, the actual classroom conditions, the actual outcomes. Let me be more concrete.

The raw data of the Cyril-Burt study or the Jules-Nielsen J. Shields study or any of the other twin studies that provide the primary data for the so-called genetic explanation for IQ have been examined by very few people. Yet it's very important to see the data in the original form. You must do a surgical dissection of these so-called "fundamental studies." From such treatment emerges the realization that, among other things, Cyril-Burt and J. Shields appear to have taken liberties with the data. For example, Shields reported as twins who lived apart a pair who lived next door to each other and have been raised by sisters.

In another case, twins discovered each other on the playground and, after that, were told that they were related; even though they lived in different parts of a small town, from then on they were inseparable. Not only that, Cyril-Burt reports in the literature, in two different cases, information that just could not possibly be true: correlation coefficients that are reported to three decimal places and do not change over ten years despite the addition of thirty studies.

Leon Kamin is very kind to Cyril-Burt. He suggests only that "Wherever one turns in his data, there are certain inconsistencies," a scientific way of being nice. Based upon those studies, quoted over and over again as the basis for estimating the inheritability of IQ, we have been trained to think about IQ and have repeated these conclusions to other people. We have been affected in our thinking by faulty data. Dr. Kamin, chairman of the Psychology Department at Princeton University, recently published a book, *The Science and Politics of IQ*.[1] If you are unfamiliar with Kamin's work, I'd like to point out that it's a symptom of what has happened to us in our training institutions. I'm as victimized as you are by some of the information and skills that have been taught. He had a hard time getting the book published, but I assure you it is a real contribution. There is abroad in the land, among people like Arthur Jensen at Berkeley and William Shockley at Stanford, among others, a perspective that has pervaded educational thinking, even among those considered friends of every child and group. These people have been misled by some of the things that pass for scientific assessment. I think, if you have not read Dr. Kamin's recent book, you owe that to yourself and to every child for whom you work.

Another thing affects all of us in the way that we perform our duties. Let me illustrate. The title of Kamin's book is *The Science and Politics of IQ*. Why "politics"? It is interesting that many of the people who are the "children" of Terman do not know what the sociopolitical beliefs of Professor Terman were. Among them are statements that blacks, Indians, Chinese, and others are members of adolescent races in incomplete stages of development. Further than that, Terman's associates included a number of people of like mind who were major names in the field of psychology. Thorndike, for example, became President of the American Psychological Association. Others, like Carl Brigham, Yerkes, Goddard are names that you all know. However, what you probably do not know—in all my training in psychology, no one ever told me, and I doubt that anyone ever told you—is that many of the leading professionals who were active at the time that the Stanford-Binet was developed also were active in an organization called The American Eugenics Research Association. They published a paper called the *Eugenics News*. Many joined the Galton Society and were joined by a number of experimental psychologists who were the top people in the field. If you know anything about history—and as educators you should—you know what our country was like around 1900. People did not simply become passive members of those societies. Those societies had certain sociopolitical functions. One such function was to lobby in Congress to pass selective immigration laws. Here is what Leon Kamin reveals about the people we learned from. They had an agenda, in addition to testing. Let me just share this with you:

> Louis Terman from Stanford, active advocate of limiting immigration from parts of Europe, based on IQ test scores, was also an advocate of selective breeding in the United States based on IQ scores...
>
> Robert Yerkes from Harvard saw IQ tests as ways of guaranteeing the place of individuals in society...
>
> Henry Goddard saw pauperism and crime as related to IQ...
>
> Carl Brigham of Princeton, through his research in reading, pointed to Nordics as rulers, organizers, and aristocrats while Alpine Europeans were described as a race of peasants, the perfect slaves...
>
> Carl Brigham became secretary to the College Entrance Examination Board and developed the *Scholastic Aptitude Test*...

Harry Laughlin, a secretary of the Eugenics Research Association, in the early 1900s became an expert eugenics agent of the House Committee on Immigration and Naturalization of the U.S. Congress . . .

E. L. Thorndike became a charter member of the Galton Society, nine people who formed a lobby for eugenics kinds of things . . .

It is interesting to note that, in 1922 when Henry Goddard administered the Stanford-Binet intelligence test to immigrants, some remarkable results were obtained in support of arguments for restricted immigration. The test results established that 83 percent of the Jews were feebleminded, that 80 percent of the Hungarians were feebleminded, that 87 percent of the Russians were feebleminded. Such results do not even need a second look. Many people don't know what these tests were developed and used for. If you did, you could understand, especially if you did an item assessment on the test, why they yield certain kinds of results.

Kamin quotes from the minutes of the Galton Society on April 5, 1920. On that date, it adopted an official statement on the maintenance of immigration control: "The Galton Society appreciates the fact that the essential character of every nation depends primarily upon the inborn, racial, family endowments of its citizens." So Jensen and Shockley take their places in a line, rather than at a new point in the eugenics fray. We see that professional people who claimed to be scholars had already reached the same conclusions. This explains why some of the prevailing bias exists today.

But this historical background is less important than what is happening now. The historical context helps us to see why we achieve some of the assessment results that we do today. Some of you know that there is now an organization called Bay Area Association of Black Psychologists. Its members recently participated in the NAACP suit that resulted in Judge Peckham's decision, a decision that has troubled many people. But I think that it offers a ray of hope for all of us, because it may make us more professional than we have been. I speak of the case of Larry P.

You may not know why Judge Peckham was able to rule in favor of the plaintiff.

Dr. Jerry West in our Counseling Department, Dr. William Pierce, and a number of black psychologists went into classrooms where pupils had been labeled retarded or educationally handicapped based upon IQ test results. Their school placement was also based on those IQs. What the investigators did was to administer the identical test but in a nonstandard way. They refused to accept a child's "I don't know" response at face value. Of course, in standardized testing, this is not permitted, because you must administer the test exactly as specified or the results are "not valid." However, it was only through nonstandard use of a "standard" instrument that they were able to discover that all of the pupils tested were average, some even well above average, even though all had been labeled retarded. This justified, with the same instrument, the assertion that they had been erroneously placed solely on the basis of an IQ test score. Some people have said, "If you take away the test, what do we do?" Please don't mistake me. We need to do real assessment. However, I don't think we've been doing that. We've been doing somethings that we label assessment, but that have been shown to be seriously in error over and over again. We need a change.

How does this tie into mainstreaming? We have stringent selection processes that identify people as cognitively different. In addition, we have less stringent assessment processes to identify people who have obvious physical handicaps. But the question is the same in either case. What is the "mainstream"? What do we mean when we say "mainstream"? One of the things that has been very interesting to me is how people in Africa and Europe are able to function in public school systems without making *a priori* judgment or without giving standardized tests to pupils. They're able to teach very well without tests, without ever making predictions. Why is it necessary, on September 1, to make a prediction about how a pupil is going to function for life, for the semester, or even for that week? It simply isn't necessary! This is especially true if the prediction doesn't work. But even if it did work, why is it necessary? How does it change the way teachers approach pupils? *There's almost no relationship between the things assessed on tests and how teaching strategies are developed.* As a matter of fact, most people don't even want to give the tests. They don't have the background to understand the tests, to interpret them to pupils, to use them in any way. In other words, they don't have the technical background to understand fully the test items or the tests' validity and reliability. We all use rough tests that we construct for courses we teach. However, that's far removed from a clinical understanding of the utilization of standardized instruments for assessment.

We get into a real bind because of the needs of the assessment industry and the shortage of money. We need a ten-dollar event that we call a test that can do everything for us because we do not have the money to do the rest. We want to be able to use a paper-and-pencil instrument for IQ assessment to find out everything we need to know. It can't cost more than ten dollars because we have mass-production considerations about which to be concerned. We can't have variable questions on our test because we think that it is important to compare New Yorkers with San Franciscans. We get into trouble because we require "standardization." This prevents us, actually, from finding out what there is that is important to know about pupils.

I happen to believe that special educators, in spite of all the difficulties, probably are better positioned to remedy the situation than anyone else in the educational establishment. But we haven't done that yet. What is it that you see when you look at test results? I'm amazed at the number of people who have never even opened a test and examined the actual items.

There is an excellent analysis of a reading test done by some teachers, students, and professors in Temple University's teacher-training project. They finally decided that, rather than accept at face value the test scores that purported to measure reading, they would take a systematic look at the test items and try to figure out what was happening with pupils. One of the things they found was that "reading," on this particular test, meant "comprehension," "vocabulary," "auditory discrimination," "beginning and ending sounds," "blending and sound discrimination." If that's what "reading" is, that gets you into a problem. What happens when you get a pupil who can understand the sentence but who cannot "read" according to the requirements of the test? Let me give you an illustration. Take four words: *like, will, it,* and *ride*; which one of the latter three words has an *i* with the same sound as "like"? This cannot be answered by a pupil from Texas if he grows up where I was born. The pupil from Texas cannot answer the question and get it correct. The problem is—if you grew up where I did—that the word is not "like" at all; it is pronounced "lak." So our Texas pupil could not possibly get the right answer because of his natural pronunciation style. Yet this is part of what, in the total score, becomes a measure of "reading." The same thing is true of the word *may.* Which word has a sound like the "ay" in *may* from among these three: *man, cake,* or *my*? If you come from where I was born, you couldn't get that right either because the word *man* is pronounced "mayn," not "man." So, the test is biased to begin with. Any person who considers himself a professional should be able to identify this situation immediately or use this information in a manner appropriate to the unique situation.

This has implications for what we do about mainstreaming, since mainstreaming is often based on a pre-assessment that indicates if a pupil should be outside or inside the mainstream. For three years I taught in a university program for the so-called gifted. We picked students for the gifted program on the basis of their College Board scores. The only problem was that, every time we gave a test, we found that we still had a very wide range, a range almost as wide as in any class on campus. The students were gifted in terms of the definition used, their College Board scores. In some cases, they were not gifted but simply glib. There is a difference between giftedness and glibness. To see which, we must look much more closely.

If you are a special educator, you'll know about such work as that of Rosalie Cohen on cognitive style.[2] I think she's done some profound things explaining to us about different people's styles of relating to the world. These styles may create dissonance in the schools, not only among minority ethnic groups, but among everyone. I'm thinking particularly of her distinction between people who have a "relational" orientation and those who have an "analytical" orientation. There are people who prefer to relate to wholes

63

or global aspects of a situation, and there are people who like to relate to small pieces. Nothing is wrong with either one; it is simply a matter of style. Rosalie Cohen suggests that the special socialization pattern derives from within the family. Whatever the origin, styles can be consistently identified clinically. People can be categorized according to their predominant styles. If you happen to be relational globally, you're dysfunctional with the schools. The things that schools ask for are highly specific, minute things. Research has shown that the way analytical types respond to a *Thematic Apperception Test* (TAT) would be to look at the TAT picture and respond to some minute piece of it. "What's wrong with this picture?" "Well, the table doesn't have a leg on it." A person with another style of approaching the world would look at the same picture and respond more globally. "Well, the chair and the table don't look good together." Those are two different styles of relating, not necessarily wrong answers. Both are equally complex. Abstrations can come from either.

We haven't known a great deal about styles. We must be very careful what we ask of pupils in school. What we ask for most often is small bits of information in multiple-choice tests. We seldom ask anyone to do global things. As a result, we bias the whole situation in schools against certain kinds of people. I saw that very vividly in terms of the people we called gifted at the university. The students who were majoring in physics and chemistry were very much ill-at-ease with what we were doing. For example, when they enrolled in a course in economics or literature, where things could not be nailed down, they were impatient. They sometimes became angry at verbosity. Their test responses tended to be short and cryptic, but very good.

Our role as professionals should not be to provide raw data for people who enjoy computer games or statistical puzzles. Our role should be to help teachers to develop skills in assessing the *clinical* situation. Special-education professionals ought to help teachers find all sources of relevant information. Unfortunately, a number of people who have information regarding what kids are doing and what they can do are systematically overlooked. Our tendency is to seek assessment data in the easiest way. Usually a standardized test is désirable because it can be done quickly. However, major contextual data about the whole experience of pupils is missed. For example, if you ask a pupil a question and your purpose is to discover if he is capable of forming a generalization, extrapolating, or making immediate inference, why must these performance functions be acceptable only in the limited mode of a narrow test question? A standardized test might not permit us to find out if the student can perform the function. The test will indicate only that he can perform the function with the data that we decided in advance would be acceptable. The same operations might be performed by a pupil with "nonstandard data," but there is no way to credit this student with the skill that he or she may actually possess. This would be a minor point, except that, in my experience, in most school districts, I'm always referred back to standardized test data as the basis for pupil placements. I wish that I could be confident that professionals who assess pupils had the requisite sophistication and understanding of the limitations of tests and also had the additional clinical laboratory skills for valid assessment. If that were the case, I would expect to see different patterns of pupil placement than now obtained.

I would like to review for a moment a few assumptions that cannot be met but that are actually a requisite for the use of IQ tests or any standardized test. I will state them grossly for emphasis. First, to use a test, you must be able to say that every child understands, in exactly the same way, the test questions being asked. If one person hears one question and another person hears a different question, you can't be certain what you're measuring. To use a test, you must be sure that the psychological constructs that are puportedly being measured, such as "intelligence" and "cognition," are culture-free. You must assume that the child's cognitive functioning is observable only through the language of standard culture and only through the value framework of standard culture. For example, on certain IQ tests, pupils must believe that women are weak and need help and that policemen are always friendly and supportive in the community. If a pupil gets a "wrong" answer, how does the examiner distinguish ignorance from disagreement?

Another assumption is that all people have the same experiences and therefore that the same information can be assumed as a data base for everyone. You must also assume that the child's thought-processes grow more complex with age. But we haven't proved that, despite Piaget. We have demonstrated only that our way of asking and the pupil's code for responding about what he can do grows more complex with age. And, there is a great deal that we don't know about what mental capacities are operative even at birth.

You must assume that testing is neutral, objective, and nonpolitical. You must assume existing cognitive tests identify, for example, *creatively* gifted students. The thing that's interesting to me is that in selecting pupils for gifted programs, we always go back to IQ tests that tend to select *conforming* pupils. Yet we know that gifted pupils tend to be nonconforming and to confront adults and authority. We describe programs in ways that are at variance with the variables being measured. Still we go back to tests. We do not have alternative ways for assessing the behavior we seek. To this point, I have seen nothing in the area of standardized testing that I find particularly useful. Some alternative assessment strategies tied to specific kinds of purposes do have much promise. But more than that, some assumptions underlying the term "mainstreaming" indicate to me that we really do not understand what the educational process is like. Who is in the "mainstream"? I don't like the word "mainstreaming," though I think the goal that we seek of re-integrating all pupils into our regular human experience is highly desirable. I wish that we had a better word than "mainstreaming" for what we're trying to do. The concept of mainstreaming is almost at variance with what we should be trying to do. I cannot conceive of a mainstream that leaves some human out. It takes all of us to make a mainstream. There is no mainstream if handicapped people are not in it. I'm amazed that, in Africa, little kids with no legs, little kids who are blind, don't seem to have the problem of being devalued as human beings simply because of a handicap. They can cut trees; they have jobs. Most so-called primitive cultures around the world that I know of can accept such differences in people quite well, including "crazy" people. These people have a place and are included without being rejected. We have separated people out and put all the blind ones over in one place, all the hard-of-hearing in another, those with low incomes in another, those with high incomes in still another. That kind of separation is unnatural. What we're trying to do is put back together what we took apart cognitively but was never apart in reality. Let's call it something else. Those who have been thought of as "normal" or "mainstream" need as much precision diagnosis as anyone else. The curricular assumptions for the mainstream need as much precision attention as any other part.

To conclude, I believe that, in spite of the kinds of negative experiences that we've had, if we will honestly treat some of the information that is now being developed, will quit accepting blindly as fact those things that have been taught to us, will become what universities are supposed to make of us—question-askers, not answer-repeaters— if we will do those kinds of things, we will be "on target" I think that we have the tools and the techniques to make a different world, one that will not be oppressive to any children, that will be enhancing for all children, and, most of all, that will be something to make us professionally satisfied with our judgments so that we can sleep at night.

NOTES

1. Leon Kamin, *The Science and Politics of IQ* (New York: Lawrence Eilbaum, 1974).
2. Rosalie Cohen, "The Influence of Conceptual Rule-Set on Measures of Learning Ability," in *Race and Intelligence* (Washington, D.C.: American Anthropological Association, 1971).

CHAPTER 5

The IQ Test and Classification:
An Inherently Harmful Situation

Armando M. Menocal, III

At first blush, it seemed that the case of Larry P. *dealt with the subject of mainstreaming only tangentially. Larry P.* involves only the question of the continued use of IQ testing, the primary method for classifying children out of the mainstream into programs for the mildly educationally retarded. In effect we accepted the classification system as we found it. For example, "What is the mainstream?"–the question raised by Dr. Hilliard–was not challenged. The usual assumptions which support special education were taken as given in our case. For example, the assumption that special education programs are beneficial to the children was not challenged. We questioned only the proposition that those programs are beneficial to children who are not truly retarded.

However, our persepective on special education was a guarded one–one based on the premise that only some children belonged in special education.

We were very concerned about the harm that special education caused to non-retarded children. The problems are well known. There's the reduced curriculum which exists in special education classes. There are the long-range problems associated with that curriculum and the fact that movement between special education and regular classes is very difficult to obtain and does not occur very frequently. In San Francisco, special education operates as a lifetime commitment. There is stigmatization of the child; problems dealing with the lowered expectations of the teacher; the lowered expectations of the child's family; and ultimately, the loss of self-confidence for the child himself, and therefore the child's on reduced expectations for himself or herself. The consequences of mislabeling are severe.

We viewed special education as something having a limited potential for good and almost unlimited potential for harm. I think it's fair to say that, therefore, we were not very friendly toward special education because of our perspective in the *Larry P.* case.

Our focus was on the system that was used to classify children. We wished to ensure that that system, which had such grave consequences, operated fairly for all children. Thus, we looked at the role of schools as sorters of children in the area of special education and as sorters in all areas.

Schools test children from enrollment to graduation. Based on those tests, schools make important decisions and take important steps with regard to what's going to happen to that child. The primary sorting instrument for children in classes for the retarded has been and remains the standardized intelligence test. The problems associated with such tests have been covered by Dr. Hilliard. The intelligence test fills the need of educators to categorize children, and it has provided a scientific justification for a certain system of classification.

In addition, I believe, it has also effectively separated children from the mainstream of education along racial and social class lines. The evidence is certainly overwhelming. In San Francisco, almost two-thirds of the classes for the retarded are made up of black children whereas black children only constitute about a fourth of the children in the school district. The statistics statewide are even worse. That the educational system has been willing to live with this and, in effect, tolerate it, I have found in itself intolerable.

This is a racist system. That word "racist" has lost much of its impact through overuse; we used it, however, in a very serious sense. Educators, people who administer programs such as those for the retarded, have been quite willing to continue to rely on a device that they know does not properly label or evaluate black children and are quite willing to live with the consequence of that system. Indeed, the state of California today insists in using IQ tests, despite the fact that I've yet to find anyone within the Department of Education who will assert that the test is not culturally biased and fails to judge black children accurately. To me, the willingness to continue to use a device that labels a particular race as inferior and becomes the basis of argument for people like Jensen and Schockley are strong evidence of its inherent racism.

The *Larry P.* case is a frontal attack on IQ tests and the consequence of IQ testing. I don't want to spend a lot of time talking about that case except to point out the three principal decisions that have been reached in the case thus far. I think these decisions tell us of the implications of *Larry P.* to mainstreaming.

First, the judge decided that the IQ test is the primary determinant of whether or not to place the child in a class for the retarded. The decision regarding what education is best for a child is very complicated. There are many factors to be considered as part of that decision. That has been one of the reasons for the traditional reluctance of courts to become involved in the education system. I think that, beginning with *Brown* v. *Board of Education,* which first declared that segregation was unconstitutional, we have seen a trend away from traditional unwillingness to deal with the education system. Until *Larry P.* no court had been willing to scrutinize an educational decision-making process and to judge the validity of that process.

The second important decision reached in the *Larry P.* case as it affects mainstreaming was that IQ tests are culturally baised. Actually, it was very easy for the judge to decide, because the defendants, San Francisco School District and the State Department of Education, never said that the tests weren't culturally biased. We're still waiting for someone to come forward and say that IQ tests aren't culturally biased. The state keeps telling us, "Don't worry, they're going to do it some day." The case has been pending for four years, and we're still waiting. Nobody has come forward to defend those tests yet, although many people within the educational establishment still ask for the right to continue using them.

The third and, I think, very significant decision was

that misplacement in a class for the retarded can irreparably harm the child. The judge's words were to the effect that a normal child who is placed in a class for the retarded for only one month is permanently and irreparably harmed and, for that reason, the judge was willing to interfere in the decision-making process that occurs in placement of children in classes for the retarded.

Now, what are the implications of those decisions? First, it's a continuation of the trend of judicial scrutiny of educational decisions. I think we can anticipate more decisions along those lines. However, with special relevance to the education of exceptional children, it appears the courts are no longer going to automatically accept the premise that classification and separation of children is necessarily better for them. From now on, those who have benefitted from that separation—and I don't believe that it's been the children; it's been the teachers and administrators—will be called upon to answer the question: Does separation benefit the child? That's something that, before the *Larry P.* case, had never been done. It has forced educators to defend particular education decisions about a child.

The second implication is that the classification devices and processes for placement of children will also become subject to further judicial scrutiny. Obviously, that is what has happened in *Larry P.* The question is how far it will go.

In *Larry P.*, and in all similar cases thus far, that scrutiny has been limited to a determination of the racial effect of the classification or testing criteria; in *Larry P.*, it was whether the IQ test discriminates against blacks. Now the question becomes one of whether or not courts will scrutinize that process, not on the basis of its racial impact, but merely on the basis of its educational impact on children. That's a much more difficult question.

Other cases have dealt with exclusion of children from schools and with the right to an education; these cases were not based on racial discrimination, but upon everyone's inherent right to an education. These cases can form the basis for an extension of what has happened in *Larry P.* to all placement decisions in special education.

Once courts firmly conclude that each child has a fundamental right to an education, then the way will be open for the conclusion that certain decisions as to the type of education the child will receive must be made on the basis of the best interest of the child. This will require a very different form of analysis because obviously all school sorting practices are not inherently harmful. School systems have to deal with a wide variety of children and a wide variety of problems; some kind of classification or sorting must occur. Whether particular classifications are harmful and therefore deny children the right to their education is essentially an empirical and not a legal question. I think the evidence regarding this injury, which would probably be in the nature of the educational inefficiency of the system and the stigma to the child, is developing, and will eventually form the basis for a merger of such forces as parent groups, public-interest lawyers, educators, and researchers on the effects of misclassification. Ultimately, doctrines based on mere racial discrimination will attach to the entire special-education decision-making process and force those who are in it to defend the basis upon which a child is placed in a special-education class. The defense will have to say whether or not, in having done so, the teachers, the educational system, have benefitted the child.

CHAPTER 6

Placement in Special Classes: The Defendant's Viewpoint, The Larry P. Case

Joanne Condas Rabin

The Larry P. *case if purely a matter of philosophy, the kind of dispute that ought to go on in lecture halls and seminars rather than in courtrooms like Judge Peckham's.* Dean Hilliard said that "the black psychologists have a case," and of course he was referring to the *Larry P.* case. It has struck me all along, as the case of Larry P. has ground through its many hearings, that I never saw one of the parents—but at every hearing the psychologists whose affidavits are in the court record would appear. I could always feel their hostility toward someone so benighted as I who would try to present a defense for what they see as the horrible *status quo*. The reason this is interesting to me as a lawyer is that usually, in litigation, the people who are suing one another have to have the interest in the issue themselves. It seems fairly clear to me that the plaintiffs in this case really don't have that keen interest; it is rather the psychologists who stand behind them who have a point to make and they have chosen the judicial forum in which to prove that point.

I would like to underscore one major point, however. The *Larry P.* case is not decided in any conclusive fashion. It's very common in federal court litigation to find that the plaintiff's attorney is able to spend a very long time getting ready before he ever takes the case to the clerk's office and files it. When the *Larry P.* case was filed, all the expertise that was ready to be brought to the firing line was on the plaintiffs' side. For that reason, and for some others that I'll have to take responsibility for, the plaintiffs were successful in getting a preliminary injunction. All that means is that, until there is a trial on the merits of the case, certain things are to be halted, and one of them is IQ testing. No quota system was imposed, nothing of that kind, so nothing really has been foreclosed by the case of Larry P. Certain preliminary steps have been concluded.

A letter received by the Department of Education illustrates fairly clearly the consequence of a preliminary step. It has an impact on everyone with an interest in special education. This letter discusses the injunction that was issued:

> This injunction effectively sets the measurement field back about seventy years. In 1905 Alfred Binet and his collaborator, Simon, published what was to be the first reasonably objective set of scales to judge the ability of school age children. Only recently has the Stanford-Binet test been challenged. The question of ethnic differences, cultural variations and deprivation aside, the test still carries out the role of school prediction most effectively.
>
> Judge Peckham's ruling has effectively withdrawn from the professional psychologist one of the few relatively objective measures available to him. Publishers of the Stanford revision of the Binet re-normed that test and published these norms in 1972. During this re-norming process all ethnic and cultural groups were carefully integrated into the standardizing sample in order to assure equal representation, thereby minimizing cultural bias. I'm aware that the best instrument in incompetent hands may yield fallacious and/or biased results. If this is the problem, then perhaps we need to review our process of selecting the professionals with whom the decision making process rests. By analogy one might say that the carpenter who mismeasures a piece of lumber should throw

his yardstick away rather than reevaluate the process he used in measurement.

As things stand, with this injunction in force, we are unable to place a child in a program for the educable mentally retarded due to the wording of Education Code 6902.07 in which we are told that an individual test is mandatory and that this test must appear on a list approved by the State Department of Education. Since the State Department of Education has withdrawn its approval of all individualized tests to be used for the purpose of identifying children for placement in programs for the educable mentally retarded, they have effectively halted the placement process.

The position we find ourselves in is as follows: when a teacher and/or principal calls on us for assistance with a youngster whose overall level of functioning is shown to be dramatically below that of his peers, we no longer have the alternative of offering the child a more intense program in a small group setting. He will be destined to remain in a classroom of upwards of thirty children and continue to be so far removed in ability from the remainder of the group as to be singled out by his peers as dramatically different. While placement in a special day class is not always the solution to this type of problem, it at least provides an option where more intensive intervention can be given to the student for basic skills and academically oriented activities. If the child exhibits a reasonable level of social skills then we are able to provide him an opportunity to participate in the larger milieu of the school where book-type activities are not constantly singling him out as different.

The most recent terminology describes this process as mainstreaming. Without the option of special placement, the student must remain in the mainstream regardless of how polluted it may

81

be. It is not uncommon for a classroom teacher with 29 or 30 students to find it impractical, if not impossible, to pay attention to a student who is grossly unable to function in a classroom setting. Historically, this was one of the reasons we removed the child who was grossly retarded as he was often permitted to set in the corner and vegetate as the classroom teacher assumed that he would never make sufficient progress to justify special effort to accommodate him. It has only been in recent years when the enthusiastic special education teacher demonstrated that many of these students were able to make limited academic progress and often dramatic contributions in other areas, including professional sports, that the special programs for the educable mentally retarded child received a degree of respectability.

It's a sad day in the history of education when the arbitrary acts of a few can completely disrupt programs that have been developing for seventy years. It is a further distressing turn of events when one man, regardless of how well advised he is, can make an arbitrary decision which negates the efforts of seventy years of research and development. I feel certain that Judge Peckham has ruled on the legal aspects of the problem at hand but has not considered the plight, anguish and distress that his ruling will bring to children, parents and teachers in the public schools of California.

That's why I'm willing to undertake the defense; I think mine is a defensible position.

To me, three points stand out in this letter as things that make the case worthwhile from a defense point of view. First, I hear over and over and over again from people who are professionals in the field, from whom I'm still trying to learn a little something, that the IQ test is one of the only objective tools that is available. Someone for whom I have great respect suggested that, if this tool goes, perhaps we will fall back on looking at the color of a child's eyes and how he relates. Those seem to me to be subjective bases for placing children in any kind of program that it is wholly irrational to throw out the tool simply because it is flawed. I'm not saying the IQ test, or any combination of IQ tests, is perfect; but I am saying that it is irrational to discard them simply because they are imperfect. I think that's true of a great many tools we use in our various professions. Certainly the jury system is imperfect, and yet none of us lawyers would care to have that thrown out because it is a flawed instrument.

It is our contention that the IQ test is useful if administered by someone who thoroughly understands the test. I add that qualification because I get the feeling from the people I've talked with in the profession that there are many testers who don't really have full command of the instrument. I left out one point with respect to the black psychologists that I do believe is pertinent here. I have to question whether they are very skilled users of the instrument with which they chose to retest the six plaintiffs. I'm certainly no expert in testing or examining test protocols, but even I could look at the test protocols of two or three of the children, as I did, and discover something that seems to me to be a flagrant departure from standardization. It was not of the character that Dean Hilliard described. It was a procedure in scoring any of the subtests where you can score an item as a 2, 1, or a 0. The examiner wrote in "1-2" or "0-1," so that I drew the inference that the tester was saying the child's answer was somewhere between those two numbers. Nevertheless, in every single subtest, when it came to totaling the score, the highest score was always used. It seemed to me that what that suggested was that the testers were striving—and had lost their objectivity as a result—to show that these were normal children who had been misclassified. But they were doing it by gross departures from the customary standardization of the test. So, I insist that the test be administered by someone who knows it and also is able to assess the child he is testing. To me, that means someone who understands that, if he's testing children in the inner city of Los Angeles, he is testing children with whom he must be specially alert for variant responses and must take into account the cultural milieu from which that child may come. However, I'm certainly not prepared to concede that, just because someone lives in a poor neighborhood, he necessarily is deprived of all the stimuli that come to him by such means as television that are widely distributed throughout our society.

It seems to me that another thing that can be done by a skilled tester is to increase use of the nonverbal portions of IQ tests and also to use a greater variety of tests to test different kinds of mental abilities. For that reason, it seems to me that the IQ test does have a place in a mosaic used for placement. It is already the case that the Education Code requires a several-step procedure: an assessment of the child's physical health, an assessment of his home background, an assessment by his teacher of his capabilities, as well as the IQ test. It is not simply a matter of administering an IQ test so that, if a child passes, he stays in the normal class, and, if he fails, he goes into the EMR program, where he is hopelessly locked into a system that provides him nothing for the rest of his life. That's simply a construct of the imagination of the plaintiffs in this case, in my opinion.

Second, referral for IQ testing is not done in a vacuum. In any kind of school situation, I think you can ask children in a first-grade class who in the class can jump the rope, who can help himself to the bathroom, who cannot read. And by fourth grade, they can make fairly sophisticated judgments as to who always has the right answers and who never does. I heard another expert in the field say the other day that he was going around to classes to look at the EMR children who were being mainstreamed. He looked at the record of one child he would not have placed back in the mainstream. He walked into the classroom without knowing which of the children he was there to evaluate. The rest of the children were all sitting back in their chairs in rows and one child was sitting up by the side of the teacher. He asked the person who was showing him around the school, "Is that Johnny?" "Of course it's Johnny, and that's mainstreaming." If that does not stigmatize that child every bit as much as putting him in a separate classroom, I'm unable to perceive the difference. It seems to me to be a distinction without a great deal of difference. Therefore, I suggest that, very generally, the referral for IQ testing is based upon the assessment of a number of people that something is wrong with a child. This may, and probably very often does, include parental assessment that something is wrong.

Very often, the IQ test will show there is something wrong with the child, but not a deficiency in intelligence. It is dyslexia; it is bad vision; it is any number of other things. But his IQ, if you want to continue to call it that, is within the normal range. Therefore, an objective test, or relatively objective test, as I'm prepared to concede, often screens children *out* of the EMR program rather than screening them *into* it.

Mr. Menocal seems to believe that mainstreaming is only tangential to the *Larry P.* case, that it isn't really involved. Yet, from the letter I cite above, it is very clear that mainstreaming has been forced upon a great many school districts in the state of California simply because they are no longer able or willing to place children in their special classes.

I conclude with a very brief summary of what has happened to three of the six plaintiffs in the *Larry P.* case. The question is whether these children have been very much helped by the plaintiffs' efforts on their behalf, or whether mainstreaming is really doing very much for them. In the first instance, this is the only child who is still in the EMR program but who is also taking classes that are prescribed for the regular curriculum:

> _____ is in the eighth grade and attends _____ Jr. High School. Last Fall he had all B grades in his special classes. In Industrial Arts, D and physical education, C. His Spring grades were all Cs for his special classes and D in P.E. He had a limited achievement in reading but has acquired a slight recognition for some words. Progress in reading is very slow. In his arithmetic he is able to work with some success up to processes involving short division. The student becomes quite angry when faced with work which he cannot immediately comprehend. When homework is assigned for skill reinforcement, the student never returns the assignment. The student exhibits poor interpersonal relationships with his peers by being abusive and picking on the other students.

The second student is now back full time in the regular curriculum:

> He was enrolled in the seventh grade last year. His grades were: English, C; Social Studies, D; Shop, D; Math, F; Art, D; Music, B; Physical Education, F. His over-all performance is considered to be slow.

The last child is described this way:

> During the Fall and Spring semester last year as a seventh grader, the student received all Ds and Fs for grades. Absences during the Spring semester amounted to 56 days. The student has not appeared for enrollment this year.

I would like to suggest that the case of Larry P. should never have taken place, that meetings of involved people, seminars on the specific subject, are the place to air this kind of question, not a federal court.

CHAPTER 7

Emerging Placement Alternatives: Implications for Teacher-Training Programs

Leo Cain

That credential requirements directly affect the education of teachers is among the important aspects of current training programs. Some thirty years ago, when we first developed certification for special education, we were in an era of legislation by groups. The first active group in the field in this state, the Spastic Children's Society—which later became United Cerebral Palsy—was interested in developing educational programs for cerebral-palsied children. They generated legislation that provided certain benefits to cerebral-palsied children only. But under this act therapists working with cerebral-palsied children could not work with children who had polio; the law stated that they were to serve only the particular category of handicap it covered. So there was expansion of legislative coverage. Categories for retarded children and others followed, and from this emerged our categorical certification program. Because each group was adamant that its particular interests be served, a series of credentials with different course sequences was established. Categorical certification of teachers resulted in public school programs that influenced categorization and solidified it.

Once an educational program such as this becomes fixed, it is not easy to change. People become committed to their particular areas and show little concern about other areas. This was one of the great weaknesses, in my estimation, of our early programs. We did not develop communication among those teaching different types of handicapped children. Each group went its own way and developed programs aimed specifically at its own group.

The situation in the state of California is unique; there is substantial legislative mandating of certification. In many states, the legislature establishes a policy and leaves it to a board or commission to develop the specifics. In California, specifics are written into the legislation. This is the situation at the present time, under the Ryan Act (1970).

When the Fisher Act (1961) was passed, a commission was appointed to study the state's entire certification process in relation to the provisions of this act. The commission found that fifty or sixty types of credentials existed. At first, some people thought that there should be a single credential, one that had been developed in special education for exceptional children, and that all areas of special education should be covered under it. Though one credential was finally issued, encompassing several categorical sequences, it was really several credentials issued under one title. The credential structure thus actually continued to embody and reinforce the categorical approach to special-education programs, both in the way we trained teachers and in the way we conducted programs in the public schools.

We now have a third system, the Ryan Credential, named after Assemblyman Leo Ryan, who authored the bill. The Ryan system once more attempts to obtain issuance of more generalized credentials. For example, the standard teaching credential is valid for K-12. We have eliminated the categories of elementary and secondary credentials and replaced them with multiple-subject and single-subject credentials. Under this system, the credential to teach exceptional children has been designated a specialist's credential. Once again, we are asking people to change their point of view and to look at new categories. This has had an interesting effect on what we call mainstreaming and on other developments in special education.

This deemphasizing of categories derives from the Master Plan for Special Education in the state of California. The Master Plan underwent intensive study and review prior to pilot implementation in 1974. Proponents are now working for legislation to implement this particular comprehensive plan, which develops and specifies services that are expected for exceptional children.

The Master Plan fails to cover the problem of personnel, particularly the problem of certification of teachers. How should teachers be certified under the Master Plan and what emphasis should these credentials reflect? Much more effort needs to be made to study the current credential pattern. This pattern will determine, to a great extent, what happens in the colleges and eventually what will happen in public school programs.

The Master Plan includes both direct and indirect services, insures continuity from preschool to high school, and funds programs that discourage exclusion. The plan makes provisions for changing program components. It develops an overall thrust that encourages programs stressing problems of physical development, occupational preparation, personal values, problem-solving, social values, intellectual potential, and reduction of the impact of disabilities. In other words, it promotes an educational focus on abilities, not disabilities.

Such disability categories as Mentally Retarded, Visually Handicapped, or Physically Handicapped tend to emphasize the disability. In the Master Plan, we have now four general areas: Communication Handicapped, Physically Handicapped, Learning Handicapped, and Severely Handicapped. If we examine them, we find that each of these areas includes a number of former categories. For instance, Communication Handicapped includes the deaf, deaf-blind, severely hard of hearing, language handicapped, and language and speech handicaps. One might well wonder how a training institution would prepare people competent in each of these areas. Probably what we must do is attempt to make people competent technically while providing in-depth training in a specific area. A teacher may not be equally competent in each category, and it will be up to the school district to place the teacher in the area of his or her strength. The same problem exists for the Physically Handicapped, and those with difficulties in orientation and mobility.

This approach to training for credentials will require a great deal of flexibility on the part of teacher-education institutions. It will make them structure their programs on a very different base and will demand, in many of the programs in this state, some serious revisions. As a member of the teacher-education program committee of the Ryan Commission, the committee that reviews all proposals from institutions, I have read all of the proposals for special education under the Ryan Act. Given the wide diversity in what each of them emphasizes, it will be interesting to see how these programs develop.

Another problem has to be examined very carefully in terms of the Master Plan. The problem, related to the integration of youngsters into the mainstream of education, is the plan's provision for the development of resource teachers.

Under the current Ryan Act, specialist patterns were developed for the four areas mentioned, but no credentialing was developed for the resource teacher. Nothing was done about the resource teacher because there was too little agreement on the function of the resource teacher and what kind of background he or she should have. The commission felt it was not advisable to lock into a credential pattern that would define the qualifications of a resource teacher. Since the topic of certification will be raised again, I am hopeful that all institutions and school districts interested in this program will come forth with constructive and significant suggestions.

What is the role of a teacher who works in an elementary school as a resource teacher? Is the best training a generic base in special education with some competency in all areas? Is it better for the resource teacher to have depth in an area like learning disabilities with lesser background in other fields? How is this to be accomplished? I remember that one of our first large programs was certifying teachers to work with retarded children. Many times, these teachers would be sent out to remote areas where they were the only special-education teacher in the school, sometimes in the county. They became resource specialists. They would return saying they were being asked to solve a wide range of problems and did not feel qualified. All we could say to them at that time was "Do your best. You probably know more about it than anyone else." But that is not a very good answer.

If we are to broaden the concept of programing in the

schools, what are the dimensions of the problem? We have been working with this kind of problem at my own institution, where we are in the initial stages of developing a program in special education that is performance-based. We work very closely with the schools rather than limiting it to the campus. But what kind of training should teachers have if they are going to work not only with a specialized category, but with the more general problem of integration of handicapped children in the mainstream of the public or private schools? The staff has developed a learning-disabilities base that is rather broad, because we feel that the primary problem these children face is learning. The learning problems are modified in terms of some of the other disabilities of the youngsters. But how do you approach children in terms of general learning problems rather than categorical problems? That implies an approach very different from the program that existed at San Francisco State when I came, but unhappily some other college and universities in this state don't seem to have moved at all from the concept we began with then.

I hope to see all teachers given a broad generic base that will provide understanding of the thrust of the schools. I would like to see broader training in psychology, sociology, management, and even creativity included as a base before we study learning disabilities and special education. Even economics is important for teachers, particularly if they're working with exceptional children. Economics is one big issue that is being raised by the public. Why are we spending all of this money? Is it worth it? We, as teachers, should be able to respond, because there *is* an answer. It's more than just saying, "We're sorry for these people and, therefore, we're giving them more money." That is not the correct answer, and it is not a very acceptable answer.

We are now receiving requests for additional special credentials. The speech people say they cannot qualify their people to be clinical under this plan, and so they have a new credential. This looks something like the old categorical approach to speech. We have faculty members who want a special credential in mobility training. Is one necessary or not? Should it be granted apart from the other credentials? If we authorized all these additional credentials, we would be back in the same categorical structure we had before.

What kinds of things do we need to look at in terms of a broader integrative approach—you can call it mainstreaming—getting exceptional children more involved in regular schools? Let me mention a few questions for which we need answers.

One of the basic issues in broadening the base for exceptional children is not the training of special-education teachers, but the attitudes of the regular teachers and principals. Part of this whole picture are problems of understanding and feeling. If attitudes are negative, it is very difficult to do a good job. Frankly, that has been one of the problems we've faced in special education all through the years, one of the reasons we've had to come in through the "back door." We have used legislative pressure to insist that these children be educated. Consider the fact that we need mandatory legislation to provide for the education of exceptional children. At the same time, we make broad statements that the schools are to educate all of the children of all the people. If the attitude toward handicapped individuals were different, we wouldn't need mandatory legislation. Many states are still working toward mandatory legislation.

One of the basic problems of placing exceptional children in regular classrooms is to find an environment that's educationally sound for them. Who controls that environment in the regular classroom? If the teacher is negative, if the teacher thinks that having two or three of these children in her class just takes up a lot of extra time, it isn't a very good learning stiuation. You must have more than just instruction. You must have a substantial level of receptivity to insure that children become part of the total environment.

I'm afraid that the effort to provide training and experience for regular teachers is not keeping pace with some of our enthusiasm for mainstreaming. I think this is a vital role for teacher education. How are teacher-education institutions, if they're really interested, going to train the regular classroom teacher to make mainstreaming possible and functional? I've read about two or three model programs. The authors of the reports suggest that success of the program was related to the many hours that had been spent in training the regular teacher. I think this is essential.

Just placing someone physically in another location doesn't necessarily mean that he or she will profit educationally. Children can sit in a room and learn nothing. We certainly don't want children to fall between the cracks. This, I think, is one of the most significant challenges for special education. What are you going to do about it? If you talk about mainstreaming, how do you plan to develop this relationship? It won't just happen of its own accord.

Some of the resources of the teacher-education program must be shifted to this task. This means a total new look at some institutions and their programs.

Another problem is prescriptive teaching and programing, the basic elements in the mainstreaming program. Canned prescriptions developed by external specialists don't work over the long run. You must have teacher participation in prescriptive teaching or programing. The ability to develop learning strategies for particular needs should be a basic objective of teacher-education programs. In the past, we sent these people to take a course in learning, and they learned about Hull's Hypothesis. In some instances, they became more confused. How do you get teachers to observe a learning problem and say, "This is the way I think that I can handle it?" Instead of "cookbook teaching," it requires, in most instances, perceptiveness and creativity. This is necessary, not only for the resource-room teacher, but for the regular teacher. This is a responsibility of the teacher-education institution.

Through the years, education has been plagued with jargon and faddism. I think I've run across more cliches in education than in any other area of my life. We talk about the "growing edge" and people in the community ask, "What are you talking about? Why don't you talk to us in English?" Mainstreaming could have some of the elements of faddism. That doesn't mean that we shouldn't pursue it. However, rhetoric about mainstreaming alone does not make it a reality. The implementation of rhetoric is a tough job. Program change is necessary. We cannot continue programs where classification systems have categorized children improperly. The success of mainstreaming will be finally determined by the kinds of evaluation components developed. We lack, in general, the evaluation components, because they're difficult, expensive, and hard to justify. I would hope that, as we develop models, teacher-education institutions will try to build-in evaluation components.

Certainly the Ryan Commission, for future revisions of the credential program, particularly as they relate to resource teachers, should receive constructive ideas from those working in the field.

CHAPTER 8

The Houston Plan:

A Program that Works

Charles Meisgeier

The issues related to mainstreaming are very much in the forefront today. The breakdown of traditional patterns is creating great pressure within the schools, while social, political, judicial, and legislative activities are bringing great pressure to bear from without. In the past, public schools have reacted to problems by setting up a task force here, a pilot project there, a special classroom in the back of the building somewhere. It is now very apparent that system-wide changes are urgently needed. Everywhere, new strategies are being tried, new roles are developing, and new delivery systems are being implemented. From my vantage point, nearly all of them relate in some way to one or more components of what we call a mainstreaming management system. You may ask "Why?" The answer seems to lie in the interdisciplinary base upon which mainstreaming is built: organization development, systems analysis, teacher training, human interaction, educational renewal, cost effectiveness, special education, behavior modification, instructional materials, media development, computer sciences, curriculum development, continuous-progress learning, individualized instruction. You can just go on and on and on. All seem to find their point of convergence in the educational management system known as mainstreaming. For this reason, mainstreaming is related to almost every issue raised in every new program in education today.

The force driving mainstreaming has its roots in special education, but the focus of its activities is upon the renewal of the whole educational system. It is demanding the development of an adaptive educational/instructional system capable of continuous renewal. Because system renewal is the focus of mainstreaming, and because it is the urgent need of the public school system, I believe that mainstreaming will be growing in significance in the months and years ahead. That is the main point that I want to make. We are facing a tremendous task of renewing an educational system which, in many parts of the country, is dying and perhaps, in some parts of the country, is already dead.

Mainstreaming—An Eye-Witness View

When the Houston School System Plan was designed and developed I was challenged with a situation that is of common occurrence. At this time, Houston Independent School District was the sixth largest in the United States. We had over ten thousand teachers, about seventeen thousand full-time employees, and a budget that was quickly approaching two hundred million dollars. The factors inhibiting change and growth and renewal in most urban education systems in this country. Initially, I was employed by a reform board and a reform superintendent (1) to develop a new delivery system for special education and psychological services and (2) to develop a system renewal program, a broad-scale teacher education program which would introduce new instructional and behavior management systems, individualized programing techniques and the application of humane principles of applied behavioral analysis.

We had to deal with all of the problems and pressures that large districts face: old school buildings; natural resistance to innovation; high staff turnover in the ghetto areas; a high drop-out rate; the labeling of new programs as experimentation; demands for change on the one hand, and active resistance to change on the other.

Special-Education Delivery System

The special-education delivery system had become rolled in special-education programs in the district. By was grossly inadequate and inefficient to meet the demands of the 1970s. It was bogged down in so many ways that band-aid approaches became inadequate; we searched for a new delivery system. Many of the social, political, psychological, and legal issues that have been highlighted in this book forced us to take a look at the existing service delivery system. It was inefficient and inadequate at every level. In 1970, there were about ten thousand children enrolled in special education programs in the district. By applying the national statistics that are used by the United States Office of Education or the Council for Exceptional Children, we knew that there had to be at least three times more children who could profit from special education services of some kind. During the subsequent years, as we operationalized a pro-active delivery system called the Houston Plan, we were able eventually to service over twenty-one thousand children with few additional funds, teachers, and materials. We were also able to obtain program flexibility and funding so we could more creatively utilize available funds to develop a modern, effective, and efficient program. Of course, we did not claim we had developed the ultimate mainstreaming program. We developed a successful model that was unquestionably superior to the prevailing one. We are very much aware that school districts, local schools, teachers, and children have unique characteristics and environments and, therefore, our plan may not be immediately or entirely replicable in another setting. Perhaps we might not have been able to operationalize the program in Houston with a different school board or administration.

Search for a Pro-Active Delivery System

In our search for a responsive delivery system, a pro-active one, we conceptualized what we called the Houston Plan, characterized as an "integrated systems plan" for education. One of the basic underlying concepts was the belief that special education programs for exceptional children could not be changed effectively in isolation from the regular instructional program. We did not believe that the subsystem or parallel system could change without changing the total system. Total, integrated planning and programming needed to occur. Second, the plan was built on the premise that teachers can change their behavior. Third, it assumed that teachers wanted to change their behavior in order to possess the skills necessary to provide children with the basic learning experiences that they must have. And fourth, we believed all children could learn more effectively in or as close to the mainstream as possible.

In taking a systems approach to the whole problem of developing a new delivery system for special education, we realized that, to change the model, we had to get involved in all the areas associated with the program. We had to deal with the roles and relationships of a number of people who had operated for many years in certain stereotyped ways. Let us look at the regular-class teacher as an example. For approximately fifteen years, we had conditioned teachers to believe that, when they had a serious problem, they should make a referral. Eventually this referral found its way to the central office; and approximately three months later, someone would come from the central office, remove the child from the class, test the child, and confirm for the teachers that the child had a problem. If the teachers lived long enough, the waiting list would be reduced, an opening would eventually occur, and the child would be removed from the regular classroom. The whole set that had been established—that when you have a problem, call for help, and somebody will eventually remove the problem from your classroom—had to be realigned. Therapists, principals, psychologists, special teachers, and others also moved into dramatically altered or new positions and/or situations.

Changing the Regularities of the System

One of the most helpful concepts in conceptualizing the plan and developing the strategies for change came from Seymore Sarason. In his book, *The Culture of the School and the Problem of Change*, he described programatic and behavioral regularities and their relationships to change in the schools. Most of the patterns he described I had witnessed over the years in my contacts with the schools. I firmly believed that we needed to discontinue past unfruitful practices, namely trying to change behavioral regularities which are only consequences or functions of more fundamental, basic programatic issues and concentrate on changing the fundamental, basic programs that create the problems in the first place. Sarason makes the point that it is very difficult for school personnel to consider alternatives to programatic regularities. Basically, he was saying that, if you get a group of people together and you say, "We need to do something about our mathematics program," they will start looking at the textbook or groupings. It would be difficult for them to consider more basic fundamental change. For example, mathematics is taught forty-five minutes every day from first grade through twelfth grade. Maybe, math should be taught for three days or for six weeks. At the end of that period, change the schedule and move to other kinds of alternatives. I am not suggesting a particular set of changes but I am suggesting that what Sarason said is true. Educators generally and administrators specifically have a great deal of difficulty looking at the fundamental issues and programs that need to be changed and in considering the universe of alternatives to any approach. As a result, problems continue; and, many times, new ones are created.

I have visited schools in which in one wing a wonderful pilot project for individualized instruction was in operation. Four teachers were working on it and the rest of the teachers were doing what they had done thirty years ago. But the problem is that five years later the pilot project was still a pilot or had been discontinued. Innovations never became part of the normal program. One of the things that enticed me back into the public school setting was the opportunity to look at some of those fundamental basic regularities and bring about changes at that level.

Much of the change effort needs to focus on changing regular education. Special education can be changed by setting up new service and support systems. However, if the fundamental "regular class" program does not become more flexible and more individualized, if there is no continuous-progress management system, or a success oriented environment and program, then we should expect to be very disappointed with the results. We must not believe that taking a special child, and returning him to familiar scenes of failure, and removing him to a resource room for an hour a day is going to be successful. The special educator is not going to be able to perform magic in a resource room if regular teachers continue to utilize punitive or irrelevant strategies they have always used with that child for the other four hours of the child's day.

The Regular Teacher's Responsibility

In the Houston Plan, we insisted at the outset on massive reeducation programs and involvement of "regular" teachers.

1. Regular class teachers would need to be involved in every aspect of planning for their children who had unusual problems.
2. Regular class teachers would need to be responsible for the coordination of the educational plan developed for a particular child wherever that plan needed to be implemented (including resource or other special setting).
3. They would be required to operationalize that part of the child's "educational plan" which needed to take place in their own regular classroom.
4. Special problems could not and would not be handled by a specialist working in isolation. The problem would be handled by a team of people working together, bringing their skills and expertise to bear on the problem to bring about the desired changes.

A Systems Approach

We examined carefully the process and the component subsystems of the total system of which special education was itself a subsystem or parallel system. The development of this subsystem during the 1950s and 1960s resulted from the schools' inability to react positively to the pressures of parents and professionals who wanted services for exceptional children. Initially because the system could not respond, the main system set up a parallel or a subsystem known as special education. I think the time has come, now, for the main system to respond, rather than continuing with a parallel system or subsystem to handle the rejects of the main system.

We have heard many people caution us and sound the alarm that regular education must be impacted. I'd like to build on that and say that all related supporting systems must be impacted—the federal programs, the transportation system, the textbook department, and maintenance and vocational systems. For example, when you start moving toward an individualized program, you may find the textbook department always distributes thirty books to a classroom; and, if you're in a third grade, you get thirty third-grade books regardless of the fact that your children are reading at first- through sixth-grade levels. Innovations may be doomed to failure because of the "business as usual" stance of the support systems which are more concerned with their own sub-goals than they are with the main system goals which they are supposed to be supporting. All it takes is for one of the supporting systems to break down or become unresponsive to changes at the same rate or magnitude as other parts of the system and you're in trouble. Although a teacher may be taught how to use many new procedures and books, certain rules and regulations in that system may prevent implementing this knowledge.

Summarizing that aspect of it, special education and regular education may be viewed as two sides of the same coin. You cannot change one without changing the other. Further, I believe we must regard ourselves as educators rather than as special educators. A few years ago, I realized that I had to accept some responsibility for what went on in the schools, that I could no longer go over to my shack at the end of the campus teaching "specials" or stay in my box of special education and just let the whole world collapse around me. I think the problems of education are *my* problems, I think they are *your* problems, I think they are *our* problems. We need to be working together to break down the walls. We need to move boundaries around even though it may mean some role redefinition, and some anxious moments on the part of those involved. We cannot continue to say, "Well, that's regular ed's problem, or that's special ed's problem." We must become change agents; and we must share what we know about individualized management systems, diagnostic clinical teaching, and applied behavior analysis.

Texas Plan "A"

The framework for the kinds of things we did in Houston resulted from the Texas State Plan A, a process and plan similar to the California Master Plan. Basically, a blue ribbon task force generated a series of seventeen recommendations for a new delivery system. There were three main recommendations: (a) eliminate labelling and categorizing; (b) shift the emphasis from the handicapping condition and the use of child-blaming labels, to the educational needs of each child; (c) keep the child with his peers and modify the regular program where necessary.

A Conceptual Design

In conceptualizing the Houston Plan, we were helped by Maynard Reynolds' original 1962 Conceptual Framework for Special Education. He indicated that most children needing special-education services of one kind or another, were either in or close to the mainstream. The more profound the handicap or the more specialized you become, the fewer number of children are served. The more specialized you become, the more expensive the program becomes: special facilities, special equipment, lower staff/child ratio. Reynolds suggested that we move children away from the regular classroom only as far as necessary and return them as quickly as possible. Over the years, however, the "two box theory" evolved; and children were placed either in a regular class or special class.

Mainstreaming is providing us opportunities to deal with those tens of thousands of children around this country who need help but don't need to be stigmatized by means of a child-blaming process to get the help they need to stay in the mainstream. That help may come as a result of special materials or suggestions given to their regular teacher. It may come as an opportunity to attend a learning center part-time each day rather than being isolated in a special setting of some kind.

Continuous-Progress Learning: A Must for Mainstreaming

During the years I was responsible for the program, Houston's special-education mainstreaming plan was constructed on the foundation of a "continuous-progress" learning model. This principle was fundamental, as a base for our resource rooms, as well as, for the regular classrooms. This "continuous-progress" system formed the foundation for the Houston Plan. We realized that mainstreaming could never be successful as a philosophy, as an instructional system, as an efficient service delivery system, until we came to grips with several myths and misconceptions about education. The myths of grading and misconceptions about learning rate and "achievement" have perpetuated mass instruction and have had a negative impact on the development of individualized instructional systems.

We recognized that the degree of learning that takes place is a function of the amount of time required by a child to learn a task in relationship to the amount of time allowed for him to learn that task. We found that, when you vary the amount of time that you allow a child to learn a particular task and make achievement a constant and time a variable, the curriculum begins to be viewed differently. The net result of this different view is new instructional management systems that are *accommodative*. All of us are aware of the myth of grading. We know there really is not such a thing as a third grade or a fifth grade or a ninth grade. It just does not exist. Educators have been very slow in coming to grips with and dealing with this fact. We continue behaving and managing as if it does exist—taking thirty children in the fourth grade and giving them fourth-grade books and work and expecting them all to perform and compete at the same level. The entire system from grading to curriculum management seems to be based on and perpetuates these myths. Some teachers have had a high, middle, and low group working on different pages; but essentially, they are still involved in mass education of children. Mass education is inappropriate, inefficient, and in many instances, destructive.

The Houston Plan

The Houston Plan developed a management system and a training program for teachers so that they could manage a group of children effectively on an individualized basis. Basically, this program provided teachers with "proven" techniques and procedures for providing an accommodative and successful program for nearly all children within the mainstream.

In a particular school in Houston with about six hundred children, there is a particular wing which is an open wing. There were about forty-five hardcore exceptional children in that wing. Many of my colleagues from all over the country visited that wing, and I challenged them to pick out the children who were "special." They could spot the child with the visual impairment. The crippled child was noticable because of his crutches or wheelchair. But my colleagues could not pick out kids who had learning problems. Nor could they pick out those who had thick files from practically every psychiatric clinic in the southwest area of the country. Such children were functioning and coping and getting along quite well. Why? Basically, because of a change from a mass instructional program to an individualized instructional program. After individualization of instruction, the other necessary kinds of things started falling into place. In addition to individualizing instruction, this school practiced positive reinforcement, which is needed for a successful program. Children must have success so that they build success experience upon success upon success.

Peer tutors are an essential part of this type of program. We may never have adequate funds for aids or volunteers—tutor programs are better anyway! Let us look at an example. We know that nearly 80 percent of speech problems are articulation problems, and probably about 80 percent of those are rs and ss. Our specialists designed a module and taught children how to train other children to remediate rs and ss. They were extremely effective. As a matter of fact, they remediated problems in children who had been enrolled in the speech correction for two and three years. In turn, those students who had had speech problems became tutors to other children.

Area Support Team

The city of Houston was divided into six geographic areas, each with a superintendent. In each of these areas, we had a special-education administrator who provided leadership to a multidisciplinary team of support personnel. The people on this team included psychologists, diagnosticians, counselors, and special-education consultants. Development of the team was a difficult, anxiety-producing process which required a period of years. There were some difficult periods as psychologists, diagnosticians, and counselors started talking to one another, began working together and sharing offices. Initially, the psychologists were spending 98 percent of their time testing children. Three years later they were spending 98 percent of their time working as team members in a teacher-training model, providing consultation to teachers and helpful services to children, usually through the teacher. They became specialists in behavioral analysis and knowledgeable about individualized management systems. These skills became generic to all team members. Each team member could also make a contribution as a member of that team on the basis of his particular discipline.

The Houston service delivery model focused on intervention at or as close as possible to the regular classroom. Most exceptional children are already in regular classes—not special classes. Most teachers state that they already have four or five children that need help. Statistics used by USOE and CEC seem to support the findings that the majority are already in regular classes. Without ever taking one child from special education and moving him to a regular class, we still have a mainstreaming component to begin with. The interesting discovery was that, as soon as children are labeled, regardless of the label, teachers who have been working with these same children say: "It's not our problem any more," or "I can't work with him; I wasn't trained to do that." I remember one meeting very distinctly. I was explaining the program and one teacher said: "What are you talking about, Dr. Meisgeier? What kind of kids are you talking about?" When I explained, she said, "Oh, that's Billy." She shouted across to a friend, "Remember how we worked with Billy!" She and the other teacher started telling me all the things they had done with Billy. About five minutes later, she raised her hand and said, "Dr. Meisgeier, I just realized what you've been saying to us this afternoon. We've been working with Billy, but, as soon as you put the label on him, *minimally brain injured*, I thought that was such a terrible thing, something so horrible that I couldn't possibly work with him. I was already looking with a jaundiced eye expecting such a child to behave in certain bizarre ways." When that expectation begins to be set, then, sure enough, students begin to conform and respond to that kind of expectation.

Personnel Retraining

Mainstreaming services are directed toward the child in the regular classroom rather than removing the child from the classroom. In each of the 135 schools that implemented the program, a Student Resources Committee was established. It was generally chaired by the principal and it included the specialist staff of diagnostic and resource teachers. We retrained self-contained teachers, speech therapists, and regular teachers to become diagnostic teachers, resource teachers, and consulting or, as we called them, precision teachers. The participating schools, instead of having a self-contained class, now had an array of new personnel and services. Included in this array was a precision learning center and a staff comprised of the diagnostic teacher, a resource teacher, and one aide. The program wasn't financed by new money, or from surplus state funds. Basically, it resulted from a reallocation of self-contained classroom funds.

The Student Resources Committee usually met weekly. Several principals told me it was an eye-opener for them to sit and deal with learning and behavior problems at that level. When I first became responsible for the program, I found that all placement was done at the central office. As part of the new plan, the staffings were done in each local school by the personnel who knew the child best. One of the area team members also attended each meeting. Parents were invited, and the referring regular classroom teacher was there. The referring teacher would eventually be involved in helping the specialist staff develop an educational plan for the child. It is essential that the regular teacher be involved in the development of the educational plan. No staffing was conducted without the regular classroom teacher's attendance and involvement. All of the remediation can not possibly be done in a resource room alone. What happens in the other four to five hours the child is in the regular class is even more important. The regular teacher must make changes in her program according to educational plan and in close cooperation with the specialist staff in the resource room. The regular teacher signed the educational plan along with everyone else on the committee.

Precision Learning Center

Each participating school had a Precision Learning Center (PLC). Under the state law, it's called a resource room. I rejected that terminology because the kinds of resource rooms that I saw were nothing more than special classes on a miniscale, incorporating some of the worst practices of special education. No modern procedures were evident. The first major decision was that the Learning Center would become a model for individualized instruction. The learning center teacher was called the learning facilitator, and she carried a load equal to that of the regular class teacher although she did not see all of her students at one time. Children came and went during the day; the schedule was flexible; every child had his folder and plan and knew exactly what he was working on and what his objectives were. He could go to the audio-visual center in the PLC. He could work with a peer tutor, or he could go to the reading center or tape center. He would be programed to meet with the teacher either individually or in a group. I am talking about children we used to think could not possibly make it in this world because they were so retarded or had such serious learning or behavior problems. They couldn't possibly assume responsibility for their own learning. They all utilized or were involved in an individualized management system if they were enrolled in the PLC. There were very few discipline problems. The programs were very precise, very specific. The interventions were charted. There were daily measurements with time samples—precise daily measurements. The PLC was one of the major support systems for regular education. It was usually one or two classrooms in size, and many of the schools put a lot of their resources into these centers in addition to what was available from special education.

Children without problems were also allowed to use the PLC. They could earn the right to participate. For example, sixth-grade spelling tapes were used by third-grade children if they were not being used by PLC students. They were welcome to come and work at the Center as long as they didn't take a lot of the teachers' time doing it. As a result, the program did not become stigmatized. My daughter was always asking me why she could not get in there more often. She wanted to get in, of course, because she liked moving at her own rate. Back in the classroom she had to move with the group.

Learning Resources Centers

Six learning resource centers provided back-up support systems for the team and special services personnel. At these

111

centers, materials specialists taught the special services teachers how to use materials. The area support teams met there. All the diagnostic teachers and resource teachers attended a training session once each week on school time. That was our training vehicle. The special services personnel participated in training sessions there, they consulted with team members, and they were involved with materials retrieval or the production of their own materials. We had everything there that a teacher could want to make or duplicate learning materials.

The plan provided for a comprehensive array of alternative services of various kinds. The program handled children in homebound programs and in about twenty-three hospitals. The program placed school district personnel in a number of community agencies for severely and profoundly handicapped children. A Learning Skills Center for older junior and senior high school age students was developed in conjunction with the program. In summary, the Houston Plan included:

    1. Massive retraining for regular educators, special education personnel, and supervisors and administrative staff.
    2. New personnel such as diagnostic, consulting and resource teachers.
    3. New instructional management systems for regular and special education.
    4. New curriculum materials and methods.
    5. An educational planning process for each child.
    6. A system for precise daily accountability.
    7. Area support teams.
    8. Learning resource center for professional staff.
    9. Expanded programing for severely handicapped.
10. In three years, a jump in services from ten thousand to over twenty-one thousand children served.
11. Participation by representative school and community groups through a large and active advisory committee.

CHAPTER 9

Special Education in Vermont:
The Consulting Teacher Approach

Hugh McKenzie

I would like to introduce you to the consulting-teacher approach to special education that we've been working on in Vermont for several years. This consulting-teacher approach to special education provides the way to reach the estimated 11,000 Vermont children and youths who are not learning at a rate that will permit them to achieve even minimum competencies by the time their schooling is completed. This approach was conceived in 1967 as a cooperative effort of the State Department of Education, the University of Vermont, and local Vermont school districts, each playing a vital role. In this effort, the University of Vermont prepares learning specialists called consulting teachers. Each year, experienced teachers are selected to begin the two-year master's program to become consulting teachers. Candidates are chosen on the basis of teaching and leadership experience, probability of academic success, and commitment to helping children with learning difficulties.

The training program for the consulting teacher consists of a summer and two full-time years of graduate study, of which the first year is campus-based for the consulting teacher in training, and the second year is district-based for the consulting teacher intern. The entire training program is performance-based, in that each graduate is expected to master a set of prescribed minimum competencies. These competencies are sequenced within each major time component of the training program, that is, the first summer, the first academic year, and the internship year. Each graduate student must demonstrate mastery of specified competencies before advancing to the next training level. The competencies themselves are based upon our analysis of the tasks performed by on-the-job consulting teachers.

Consulting teachers are hired by local school districts to assist and train regular classroom teachers to help children with learning problems. The state and the district share the cost of hiring consulting teachers and the aides who work with them and the classroom teachers. Consulting-teacher services are currently available in twenty-five of Vermont's fifty-six superintendencies. In Vermont, a superintendency may have several school districts within it. This year over 2,000 children and youths have been served through this approach.

The consulting teacher serves all but severely and profoundly handicapped youngsters, these youngsters at this time in Vermont usually being placed in a special class or residential facility. The children served by consulting teacher are traditionally categorized as learning disabled, emotionally disturbed, or educable mentally retarded. The consulting-teacher approach augments, rather than competes with, existing programs. The consulting teacher usually teams with other specialists, such as the speech pathologist and counselor, to provide a total, integrated program for the child with learning problems.

We feel that the consulting-teacher approach has several major advantages. Among these is the fact that it is cost-effective in that it utilizes presently employed personnel and existing classrooms. It is noncategorical in that children are not labeled or segregated from the mainstream. And it is educationally effective in that the consulting teacher is accountable for accelerating learning rates.

The consulting-teacher approach is both training-based and data-based. It is training-based in that teachers are trained by the consulting teacher to provide individualized instruction. It is data-based in that precise measures of each learner's progress are recorded and analyzed daily.

In-service training for teachers and auxiliary personnel is accomplished through consultation, workshops, and university course work. Consulting teachers are appointed as associate members of the faculty of the College of Education and Social Services at the University of Vermont. This year, over 350 classroom teachers, principals, guidance counselors, and so forth have taken course work on an in-service basis from a certified consulting teacher. Up to twelve hours of graduate-level course work in special education can be applied toward a master's program in teacher education as a special-education concentration.

The consulting teacher is, we hope, a highly trained professional who is skilled in applying learning theory, writing instructional objectives, and developing specific teaching strategies. These skills are shared with teachers and other school personnel through in-service training offered by the consulting teacher. Consultation is a less formal kind of in-service training and is a cooperative effort between the teacher and consulting teacher to provide services to an eligible learner.

We operate under what we call the data-based individualized model of education. In this model, decisions are made at several key points: first, when determining the child's entry level; second, in deriving a sequence of objectives the child is expected to achieve; third, when developing specific teacher-learning procedures; and, finally, in evaluating the effectiveness of the learning program. However, before proceeding through these steps, it is necessary to determine the child's eligibility for service. Eligibility requires the classroom teacher's referral, her specification of the problems on concern, and measures indicating achievement less than that expected of age mates.

As an example, I'd like to present the model case of Larry. When Larry first entered public school, he was not toilet-trained and was sent home after two weeks. He returned a year later and, after a year of extensive testing, it was concluded that Larry was functioning mentally and physically three years below his age mates. He was labeled educable mentally retarded and recommended for placement in a day school for retarded children. Larry's deficits included some spasticity and some deformities in his legs which contributed to an unusual but functional gait. He also had petit-mal seizures for which he was taking medication. Larry's parents refused special-school placement and insisted that Larry continue to attend his neighborhood school, which was just a few hundred feet from his home. Larry was referred to the consulting teacher at this time by his second-grade teacher. The principal played a key role in managing and supporting the entire program; he also took courses from the consulting teacher. The consulting teacher in this case indicated that the principal's feedback was vital to the program (we find this to be generally true).

The next step in the model, now that we've determined Larry's eligibility, is that of determining the highest level in the instructional sequence at which the learner has achieved mastery. This is the learner's entry level and the point at which instruction begins.

The consulting teacher and the teacher obtained entry-level measures in reading and math that indicated that Larry was reading on a preprimer level and functioning on a first-grade level in math.

The next step is arranging an individualized sequence of school-year objectives that will insure achievement of minimum competencies by the learner. Minimum objectives, as we call them, represent the basic skills and knowledge that every child is expected to achieve during a given period of time. Community-approved minimum objectives represent the basic skills and knowledge that every child is expected to achieve through public school instruction. We do involve the community in approving these objectives. For the learner not achieving the objectives, the consulting teacher is expected to design and implement, with the classroom teacher, an instructional program that will accelerate the learning rate of the child to one leading us to project that the learner will achieve all of these objectives by the end of the learner's course of study in that school, or to a rate that is double that of the minimum. We've set that minimum line to represent one month of learning to one month of instruction. If you double the rate, you need two months of learning for one month of instruction.

Developing teacher-learning procedures is the next step in this model. Immediate feedback for correct responses, imitation training, timed quizzes, and contingent treats were some of the procedures used with Larry. The teacher and a part-time aide conducted these procedures daily. The consulting teacher demonstrated the procedures and observed their application to provide feedback to the teacher and the aide.

The teacher's role included one-to-one tutoring, providing group work for Larry throughout the day, and monitoring the aide. The classroom teacher met with Larry daily for a thirty-minute reading session using the Ginn 360. Her instructional program applied two learning procedures: imitation training and reinforcement. In imitation training, praise is provided for correct word recognition. When Larry did not know a word, the teacher told him the word and Larry imitated her. For reinforcement, after Larry learned all the words of a story, he was allowed to read the story to the teacher. Larry was praised for reading correctly. When he misread a word, the teacher said the word, Larry imitated her and continued reading. The teacher asked Larry five comprehension questions when he completed the reading assignment. Larry was praised for correct answers. When he gave an incorrect answer, the teacher told him the correct answer.

The aide's role included one-to-one tutoring, compiling data, and conferring with the teacher and consulting teacher. The aide implemented the Palo Alto Language Program during a thirty-minute daily session. The instructional program applied the principles of reinforcement and imitation training in a slightly different manner. Reinforcement was done by immediate correction of Larry's work. As Larry completed each page in the Palo Alto workbook, the aide marked a "C" on correct answers. Incorrect answers were reworked until they were correct. Imitation training was used when Larry orally read the Palo Alto readers. The aide praised Larry when he read passages correctly, and when Larry misread a word the aide told him the word and Larry imitated it.

The consulting teacher's role included planning for and evaluating the effects of the procedures that were employed with Larry and in training the aide and the teacher to conduct the procedures. Training procedures for the aide extended over a four-week period. After the assigned readings and written units were completed, the consulting teacher provided support and encouragement as the aide discussed the content of the assignment. They also planned specific teaching strategies to increase Larry's learning rate. The consulting teacher and aide role-played the learning situation. First, the aide acted as the learner while the consulting teacher demonstrated the instructions, recorded response, and provided the specified consequences. Then the aide performed these activities while the consulting teacher acted as the learner. When the aide performed the specified activities with 100 percent accuracy, according to the written instructions, and when the data recorded on the learner's responses were 90 to 100 percent reliable, the aide began the procedures in the classroom with Larry.

The final step in our model is that of evaluating the effectiveness of the service. Larry's entry point showed him to be at the 1.5 level equivalent. Over a five-month period, Larry completed materials through the 2.3 grade level equivalent. Larry's rate of achieving minimum objectives in the Palo Alto Program showed that, over a five-month period, he read the first five books in that series. In the Addison-Wesley Math Series, Larry's entry-level measures were at the 1.5 grade level equivalent before the program was implemented. After three months, Larry was achieving objectives at a fast enough rate to insure acquisition of all minimum math objectives by the end of the six years in this particular school.

To review the service provided for Larry: eligibility for service was determined, objectives were sequenced, teaching-learning procedures were developed and implemented, and daily measures were used to evaluate service. This is a typical example of consulting-teacher services, but there are other ways in which these services can be delivered. Some learning programs are programed beforehand and are self-administered for the learner who does not need one-to-one instruction. Some programs provide frequent contingent praise for the inattentive learner. Some programs employ management procedures for the distuptive learner. All of these programs fit into this data-based individualized model of education.

Depending on the district's needs and priorities, the consulting teacher may provide service for the elementary school, for the secondary school, or for preschool children. Elementary-level model consulting teachers are currently available in twenty-three districts in Vermont. Classroom teachers learn special-education strategies through consulting teachers in-service training programs. One-to-one instruction is provided where needed through the children's teachers or parent volunteers, aides or peers.

The secondary model is currently available in two school districts in Vermont. Services may involve special contracts with students. Daily remedial instruction may be offered in a resource room supervised by the consulting teacher. Volunteer students often help in preparing materials and correcting work. The teacher again plays a major role in delivering service.

Preschool service in Vermont is called Essential Early Education. Two school districts have such a program using consulting teachers, and an additional five school districts are served through a regional program directed by a consulting teacher. Children from birth to school age are given service in their home setting. Parents are provided the necessary materials, instruction, and support, which enables them to help their child on a daily basis to insure later success in school.

Let me now answer, in a kind of dialogue, some questions about the Vermont program:

Q: How much of the internship is paid for by the state and how much locally? What is the cost?

A: The cost of the internship year to a local district for an elementary-level program is approximately $5,200. This includes a part-time salary for the consulting teacher, salary for a half-time aide to work with the regular classroom teacher, office supplies, special instructional materials, and often a budget for travel if the consulting-teacher intern has two or more schools to go to. The state typically does not help during the internship year. The university, through a grant from the Bureau of Education for the Handicapped, provides a fellowship for the consulting teacher and a supervising faculty member who works with principals, directors of special education, and others to implement the planned program for that district. The intentions of the school district and the intern are that, if everything works out well in the internship year, the intern will be employed full time in that district. At that time, the state pays for 75 percent of the consulting teacher's salary and 75 percent of the aide's salary.

Q: Would you go over the functions of the personnel

involved in the preschool program?

A: The preschool program is home-based. An aide works in it to assist the consulting teacher and the parent, but there are no classrooms or preschool teachers as such. We look upon the parents as teachers. At the elementary level, a consulting teacher is available and a consulting teacher's aide for the regular classroom teacher. If additional aids are needed for one-to-one tutoring, the consulting teacher and the classroom teacher work together, often through the school principal, to obtain the necessary one-to-one tutoring. This may involve training peer tutors, if that's feasible, or bringing in tutors from the high school. It may mean volunteers, or, if the child has serious difficulties, the state has responded by providing 75 percent of additional paraprofessionals' salaries to serve a child. For example, we've had several children diagnosed as autistic. We've been able to maintain them in regular classrooms. Initially, these children had a paraprofessional who sat beside them throughout the entire school day to prevent them from harming themselves or other children. Eventually these paraprofessionals, over the years, have been phased out.

Q: How often are the children in the preschool program worked with, and is there a problem for the parents in obtaining access to special materials?

A: We usually hope to have the program that the parents are carrying out in the home—the preschool model—on a daily basis. Special materials and so forth would be brought to the parents and left in the home for them to use.

Q: Are visually handicapped students served under this program also?

A: For quite a long while, visually impaired students in Vermont have typically been integrated into regular classrooms. Two consultants working out of the State Department of Education provide special materials and techniques for regular classroom teachers for the visually impaired. Often the consulting teachers and these consultant specialists for the visually impaired will team together to work. But it's not specifically part of the consulting-teacher approach.

Q: Do all children learn at a specific rate, or is there a variety of rates?

A: The children themselves learn at a variety of rates.

There is one minimum rate for all children and, if a given child is not achieving at that minimum rate, that's a signal to us that we've got to do something more for this child.

Q: How often is the classroom teacher expected to spend long periods of time with a particular child, and how many handicapped children is he or she expected to take? Also, what is the workload for the aide?

A: The number of these children we would expect a classroom teacher to work with really depends on the situation. There is no pat answer. It depends on the needs of the other children in the class. It depends on the amount of deficit and the management problems that the child eligible for special education in that class presents. At times we don't expect a teacher to work with any. We really think there have to be auxiliary personnel. The classroom teacher can manage, supervise, and, with the consulting teacher, devise the particular learning program. We've had as many as eight children in one class, who were clearly eligible for special education, in a teaming situation with approximately forty other children. There were two teachers and two paraprofessionals who were hired to work with the children under the teachers' direction for at least part of the day for some one-to-one instruction. One of the consulting teacher's responsibilities is to see that the classroom teacher has the resources so that she can succeed with these special children as well as the other children.

The reason Larry's teacher had periods as long as thirty minutes per day to work with him on a one-to-one basis was that the class was involved in reading groups at that time.

Our recommendation is that there is one consulting teacher and one consulting teacher's aide per five hundred children or youths or twenty classroom teachers.

Q: How many children is the consulting teacher expected to serve per day?

A: We expect the consulting teacher in the course of the year with the aide to serve forty children or youths. Perhaps this cannot be stated in terms of any one day, because the teachers might be carrying out the programs themselves unassisted by the consulting teacher.

Q: How receptive are the secondary teachers to the special students and the consulting teachers?

A: All teachers embrace this approach with varying

123

degrees of enthusiasm. Not all welcome it with open arms initially, but usually one or two teachers are willing to give it a try. Then, once those teachers have had some success, they tend to talk to other teachers about that success, and other teachers come and look, and it spreads gradually. I think it has to be a gradual program—at least we haven't found a way to do it all at once.

Q: Have you done any evaluation of the kind of relationship between the classroom teacher and the consulting teacher that will help us understand what is involved in that relationship?

A: Evaluation, yet, in terms of the fact that more and more teachers are becoming involved in demonstrating their success, not only in providing effective and humane education for children eligible for special education, but for the other kids. The question is such a complex one, and varies so from teacher to teacher, that a pat answer would have to be suspect. The consulting teachers have a great many social skills, and they sincerely like people, particularly regular classroom teachers. They are people who have taught regular or special classes themselves for a median of five or six years. They understand the problems of the classroom teacher. They look at themselves as working for the classroom teachers. The classroom teacher has the final say in all decisions—and I think it has to be approached that way.

Q: On the secondary level, are the teachers chosen to have these special youths in their classes, or do they volunteer?

A: We like to start with a request from a teacher for help from the consulting teacher. This is particularly true when a program is just beginning, so teachers are volunteers. We like to think of it as on a volunteer basis throughout, knowing that every teacher must be involved before this program can have ultimate success but gradually working toward that goal in a way that balances the comfort of the adults involved with the learning of the children or youths involved.

Q: Is there any systematic reinforcement offered for these teachers?

A: Yes. The consulting teachers will ask the principal to see what great work Miss Jones is doing, let the parents know what great work Miss Jones is doing. There is an opportunity to get recertification credit for work with those special children and the consulting teacher and to get graduate-course work. Before we start in a district, we've done a lot of work with superintendents and principals, guidance directors, and so forth, with the school board, and with members of the community, as well as with the teachers themselves. We let them know what the program is, answer their questions about it, and give them an opportunity to discuss what kind of relationship they might like with the consulting teacher, whether consultation, workshops, a course, or all three, and when they would like to begin. We ask them what children and youths they would like some help with.

Q: If and when government funding is curtailed, how do you foresee the funding of the project?

A: I think I'm fairly optimistic. Most of this program is funded by within-Vermont monies. The only without-Vermont monies that we have are the Bureau of Education for the Handicapped fellowships. It is my opinion that the state itself would provide those fellowships if BEH were to go away.

Q: If a consulting teacher has forty children for whom she is responsible, how will she apportion her day?

A: The consulting teacher spends most of her day in regular classrooms. One joy of the aide is to take over the class for the regular classroom teacher while the regular teacher and the consulting teacher confer. Music periods and physical education periods can also be used as conference time. Fifteen or twenty teachers don't all start a program right at the beginning of the school year with the consulting teacher. Teachers are at different stages in the program. If the teachers are taking a workshop or a course, these almost invariably involve serving a child eligible for special education. The consulting teacher is then really consulting in a group situation which is economical.

Q: How do parents of children who are not in the special program feel about all this extra time and attention being given to those who are in it?

A: Generally they feel very good about it when it's explained to them. They can observe what their child is learning, and their child often will benefit from the new skills that the classroom teacher is acquiring. After a year or so, when districts have set up their community-approved minimum objectives, at least for the reading and arithmetic areas, many schools have changed their report cards and they report to parents with graphs or with narrative descriptions of graphs. And all parents are very enthusiastic, and the data show that the other children are benefitting from the new skills that the classroom teacher is acquiring.

Q: Are the parents involved in the determination of the minimum rate of achievement?

A: Yes. In the consulting-teacher approach, the parents are involved every step of the way. When the referral is made, the classroom teacher and the consulting teacher will meet with the parent and explain why the referral was made; the parent must sign a letter of informed consent agreeing to these services. The parent agrees to the teaching-learning procedures that will be applied and also checks on the relevancy of the sequenced instructional objectives that will be the immediate learning goal of the referred child. The parent is given feedback, evaluation data as to how the child is progressing, and the parent is given the opportunity to have help if he or she needs help in management at home or wishes to supplement the teaching of reading by carrying out some procedures at home. The objectives themselves and the time-frame that lead to the minimum rate are usually set up by the entire staff and the principal of a given school, with involvement of the school board and as much of the community as the school board can be encouraged to entertain.

CHAPTER 10

How to Fail in Mainstreaming without Really Trying

Robert H. Bradfield

During the past decade we have witnessed a dramatic increase in the demand for the implementation of procedures which more effectively provide for the educational needs and more adequately protect the constitutional rights of handicapped children. Growing out of the civil rights movement of the late sixties, this emphasis, popularly referred to today as mainstreaming, has resulted in a need for a major reevaluation of all facets of education. As has been the case with the demands of any minority group for equal protection under the law, this movement has resulted in reactions ranging from willing support and commitment to consternation, fear, and confusion. In part, resistance stems from an assumption that mainstreaming will occur within the confines of regular educational programing as we know it today. Obviously, this cannot be the case. If mainstreaming is to succeed, present-day classrooms must be modified dramatically to accommodate not only the handicapped but the children who are already there as well.

As one who has both succeeded and failed in attempting to implement mainstream programs, I would like to describe some of those changes I feel must occur if we are to prevent this "mainstreaming" effort from failing and thus resulting in further restriction of the rights and guarantees of the constitutional heritage of both handicapped and normal children.

Least Restrictive Alternative

If we are ever to implement both our legal and moral obligations to the handicapped successfully, the first step must be one of clarifying and objectifying the terminology under which we operate. Recently, court decisions have focused upon the concept of "least restrictive alternative," which has essentially been interpreted as meaning regular classroom placement. Although this interpretation may well apply to the majority of handicapped children, given appropriate supportive services within the regular classroom, it would appear rather naive to assume that the least restrictive environment for any given child, though not infinite in number, may cover a range of possibilities of both temporary and long-term educational intervention and/or therapeutic treatment. Needless to say, a statement such as this immediately acts to offer an out to the opponents of mainstreaming and raises the possibility that the least restrictive alternative may become the next great area of misuse and misinterpretation in education. Unless we can develop objective means of determining what is, in fact, "least restrictive" for any given child, the interpretation of least restrictive alternatives is in danger of becoming even less controllable than deciding the meaning of terminology such as "EMR," "LD," "EH," or any of the other categories into which we have arbitrarily placed children and then, interestingly enough, changed those categories as such change became expedient.

Those who "believe" that the least restrictive environment for handicapped children is the special class will undoubtedly continue to so interpret the needs of children, while those who "believe" that the best place for the handicapped child is in the regular class will continue to interpret according to their perceptions. In neither case will we have an objective, child-data-based system that allows placement on the basis of clearly observable and verifiable information.

Benefits to Regular Education

Mainstreaming must, if it is to take into consideration the rights of all children, establish a process by which not just the handicapped alone, but all children in regular classes may benefit. If we first recognize that there are at least as many, if not more, handicapped children already in regular classes who have never received special help, who have never been provided with appropriate individualized programs; and if we recognize the rights of the "normal" and/or the "gifted" child to achieve his or her potential, then we must also recognize that any mainstreaming process must provide for these needs.

Pre-Service Training

If the mainstreaming effort, with all the concomitant benefits that can accrue from such efforts, is to be anything more than a temporary palliative, it is essential that those institutions of higher education responsible for teacher-training programs at all levels of "regular" and "special" education must effect major changes in their structure and content. The first and perhaps most important step in this change is the breaking down of those territorial boundaries that we, as educators, have established, either for our protection or to enhance our own self-esteem. The empires of special education, communicative disorders, elementary education, secondary education, and on and on must give way to a social order in which it is recognized that individual education is not the protectorate of any group. There are not stone tablets that must be delicately guarded, either for groups of children, levels of children, or special characteristics of children. Special education is not special. When one gets beyond prosthetics, the principles taught are no different than those which are or should be taught in every other area of education. The old notion out of which special education has grown that groups of children are, in fact, different in terms of their learning processes, can no longer be tolerated. By the same token, the emphasis of elementary or secondary education upon the attributes and learning abilities of "normal" children with the "special" child's needs left to the special educator must be discarded. The day of separate departments each housed in its own building or its own part of the building is over. Cross-fertilization and the mutual use of skills must begin. The content of our courses must be carefully reexamined and made dependent upon child-data-based evaluation of their effectiveness. It makes no more sense to build a program for slow learners in isolation. The sooner we recognize that much of our exclusiveness is designed to protect our own creature comforts, such as who has what secretary, who gets what travel funds, or who gets to make what decisions, rather than to determine how our training program can eventually benefit the individual needs of children, the sooner we will get to what mainstreaming is all about.

Funding

Funding of educational programs for handicapped children over the past two decades, still based primarily on the "sympathy" approach, has increased dramatically, though in many cases there is no rational basis for the wide funding variations from state to state and even program to program. Nevertheless, one must recognize that, in general, legislatures of both federal and state governments have responded quite generously. Interestingly enough, however, because of the emphasis in the past on pull-out programs with separate environments established for the handicapped, the funding that is being generated now becomes one of the principal roadblocks to the mainstreaming process for at least five reasons. First, most legislatures have made funds available only for children placed in separate environments. As a result, those laws designed to aid in the education of handicapped children now become financially punitive if the child is returned to the mainstream of education, even though at least as much money is required for appropriate placement in a regular-class program as was required for special-class placement. Second, there appears to be a great deal of fear among special educators that the more we emphasize the right of the handicapped child to educational opportunities with his less handicapped peers, the more we jeopardize the funds that have been made available. Third, the careless and unintelligent application of mainstreaming that can be observed where financial economy rather than the individual needs of children has become the primary concern has alienated many educators. Fourth, in many cases the establishment of special programs for the various categories of special children has also resulted in the establishment of administrative hierarchies related to the operation of these programs. Freeing funds from the special-class restriction therefore threatens this administrative hierarchy with loss of positions, since, if a child can be adequately mainstreamed, he or she will, in all probability, aslo fall within the administrative domain of regular school administrators, assuming that these administrators are appropriately qualified. And, finally, fifth, the return of the special child to the regular class implies that fewer funds will be available or necessary to pay teachers of special-class programs.

It is essential that future funding be based not on the ability to instill sympathetic reactions in our legislators via billboards, etc., but must be based on the constitutional right of all children to education appropriate to them and the realistic costs of providing that education. Funding procedures that restrict the availability of funds to those children placed in separate environments must be changed to allow for an effective mainstreaming process.

Curriculum Delivery Systems

Historically, a major impediment to the provision of individualized instruction within the regular classroom has been the lack of availability of effective curriculum delivery systems that would allow teachers to provide appropriate level materials for each child in his or her classroom on an individual basis. The almost overwhelming task of providing an individualized curriculum for each child in a class of thirty children in four or five different subject areas daily has yet to be realistically considered. Learning centers are not the total answer, programed instruction is not the total answer, grouping is not the total answer. Rather, we need to prepare teachers with careful training in the effective utilization of the best aspects of all of these. We need a greater abundance of carefully sequenced, child-tested materials in all subject areas that can be selected from and prescribed on a daily basis without keeping teachers up until midnight doing so. Instructional programs are of little value if the end result is an exhausted teacher who can no longer maintain the system. I recall being in a setting in which we developed what proved to be a very effective individualized instruction program and having teachers say to me, "It's wonderful; the children produce three times as much as they produced before. They learn far more rapidly, but I would certainly like to see my husband/wife once in a while." This is not an effective individualized system.

Fortunately, a good deal of groundwork has already been done in this area and several models are available which can be built upon. However, the work is far from complete and requires a major emphasis if we are to be successful.

Teacher Consequences

During the past decade, with the gradual increase in acceptance of the behavioral philosophy in education, a rather interesting contradiction has occurred. Though we are quite willing to recognize that children need appropriate stimuli and appropriate consequences and that, given these conditions, performance and learning will increase rather dramatically, we have somehow denied the same principles when it comes to teacher behavior. We have assumed that teachers do not operate according to these same principles; rather we assume that they will understand on a rational basis anything done educationally, whether rational or irrational. This "you'll get your reward in heaven" philosophy has resulted in a great injustice to many highly qualified teachers. If mainstreaming is to be a success, it is essential that we recognize that the same principles of learning that apply to children apply to their teachers. We can no longer continue to give the teacher who is good at handling special problems all the special problems while avoiding burdening the teacher who is poor at handling such problems. By so doing, we inadvertently punish good special-problem-teaching behavior. Even those model mainstreaming programs which have developed over the years have failed to recognize the hidden consequences for teachers in such programs. Just being designated a "model teacher" and having one's classroom constantly visited and held up as an example of special-teaching effectiveness may provide social reinforcement to teachers so involved. However, when an attempt is made to extend the program to other classrooms and we simply ask teachers to engage in the same program on a very routine basis, we often see programs fail because such special reinforcers are now removed. It is essential that we recognize that mainstreaming of handicapped children can become an adverse consequence for teachers in whose classrooms these children are mainstreamed simply because they add one more increment of work to that teacher's load without ever providing a balance of positive consequences. Any mainstreaming effort must provide teachers with this balance in the form of additional resources, both human and material, to counteract the additional workload placed upon them.

Too often we have simply focused upon changes in teaching behavior without considering accompanying change in teacher attitudes. Such attitudinal change is crucial to the success of the mainstreaming effort and is not likely to occur if the special child is continually seen as a greater burden and therefore even more special. The regular classroom teacher needs the resources and the time to deal with the unique demands of each child in his or her classroom and through successfully meeting such demands to begin to recognize the similarity of the special child to those other children with whom he or she deals. Currently, all consequences in special education are in favor of pull-out programs. Funding, reduction of classroom problems, child/teacher ratio, and so forth, all favor special class placement. Somehow this process must be reversed.

Dependence on Personalitites

While there is no question that any effective educational program requires strong leadership in combination with group involvement, there has been a tendency in the development of many model mainstreaming programs to build programs inadvertently around the unique personalities of individuals without making appropriate provision for the transition to a time when those individuals will no longer be present. Procedures, resources, personnel positions, both teaching and administrative, must be organized in such a way that effective mainstreaming will continue despite changes in personnel, even to the extent of tolerating and taking into consideration the possibility of some individuals who may be less competent than might be desirable.

Child-Data-Based Intervention

The time should be long past in education where interventions that take place, placements that may be made, whether in regular or special classes, or decisions that are reached can be made on anything other than hard behavioral data, monitored continuously for appropriate periods of time. Returning children to regular classes without careful documentation of their progress in those classes is no more acceptable than the placement of children in special classes without documentation of the effect of that type of placement. Unfortunately, we have been guilty in both regular and special education for many years of just such practice. It is essential that we begin to demand of all those companies who publish the textbooks we adopt, of all those companies who publish tests we use, and of all those universities who train the teachers on whom we depend, that each be able to present child-performance data each step of the way that demonstrates the effectiveness of their product or program. It is time that we begin to document why specific school policies and procedures have been initiated and to produce supporting child data in order that we may be assured that such policy is for the child's benefit and not simply institutional expediency.

Parent Participation

We are currently in a facinating period of legal challenge to educational tradition in which the parents of handicapped children play a major role. The number of court cases and legal decisions is increasing dramatically. We find some parents bringing legal action demanding recognition of their child's right to education within the regular classroom, while others are bringing suit and initiating legislation to establish special self-contained programs for those with unmet needs. Still others are bringing suit because of diagnostic change—the movement of their child from one category to another. Almost unanimously, parents are demanding access to information and the right to be included in the decision-making process. And yet we often proceed in our mainstreaming activities as though our will was the parents' will. Evidence to date does not suggest that parents of handicapped children favor mainstreaming. In a recent study by Ariel, 59 percent of parents of learning-disabled children sampled indicated a preference for a special self-contained classroom for their child; 21 percent preferred regular class half-time and resource room half-time. Regular-class placement with tutorial help was preferred by 15 percent, while only 3 percent indicated a preference for simply regular-class placement. Apparently, these parents do not share our negative perception of the special class and our commitment to mainstreaming. It would appear that the burden of proof is on us. Not only must we demonstrate the efficacy of mainstreaming to these parents; we must include them in planning and implementation. Who has a better right? It is their children's lives with which we experiment.

Stop the PR—Be Honest

We all have a tendency in our enthusiasm—and perhaps to protect our individual images—to focus upon our successes and present the rosiest of portraits of mainstreaming programs with which we have been involved. Somehow, in this process, we overlook our failures, gloss over continuing problems, and omit discussion of design weaknesses. In so doing, we fail to provide our audiences with perhaps the most important data any project generates, the pitfalls. It is time that we admit to less than perfection and in conjunction with our slide shows and PR movies provide detailed analyses of the dark side of the moon. Otherwise, we may simply perpetuate systems with the same frailties they have always had. The first place each of us must look is at ourselves and the part we played in those difficulties. For example, the North Sacramento Project was a failure! For three years we successfully mainstreamed handicapped children and improved the educational environment of normal children. Then federal funds ran out—and so did the project. One of our teachers now teaches in a self-contained special class, and the others are off doing something else. We had built a system that required too much from teachers, that was too dependent on individual personalities, and that lacked commitment to continue without additional funding even though alternatives were available. Unless these factors become part of our presentation of the North Sacramento story, we present a misleading and inaccurate portrait of the mainstream process. Let's learn from our failures as much as from our successes. Our job is to educate, not indoctrinate.

Quit Making Excuses

It should be clearly emphasized that the lack of one or more of the previously stated conditions should not be used as an excuse for failure to build appropriate mainstreaming programs. This is not to imply that each of these conditions is not an important consideration for effective mainstreaming. It simply means that a great many effective programs have been initiated lacking many of these prerequisites. Instances abound of successful mainstreaming efforts with a wide variety of handicapped children without appropriate pre- or in-service training of teachers, without appropriate funding, without committed administrators, without additional resources, and without additional positive consequences for teachers. In all probability many successful programs in the future will also lack many of these strengths. We must not wait until all things are perfect, for it is doubtful that they ever will be, before we begin to expand the mainstream process. Through this process the university academician who insists on continuing to teach "The History of Cretinism," the school administrator who blames everyone except himself for failure to mainstream, or the teacher who tries to exclude every child with whom she or he has failed will be overcome. These are conditions to be achieved, not prerequisites. We must start with as many such conditions as possible and, through a successful mainstreaming process, attain the rest of them as lasting conditions in education. The rights of children may not be set aside until all factors that prevent attaining these rights can be satisfied. Special children are first and foremost children, with all the uniqueness and individuality that the term implies. Unquestionably, their special needs must be met, but our efforts must be directed toward modifications in the natural environment that will allow meeting these needs rather than the process of segregation on which we now depend. Attempting to teach "normal" behavior in an "abnormal" environment is incogruous. By so doing we lose all the richness, all the variety, all the subtle shades and tones that one's peers of all colors, shapes, sizes, strengths, and frailties provide. We teachers are part of the educational process and must never forget that it is we who must respond to the demands of children, not children who must respond to our demands. The mainstreaming process can be the essence of what education is all about. It provides us with the vehicle to achieve the individualized instructional system to which we have given lip service for so many years by allowing us to meet the special needs of the handicapped while more effectively meeting the special needs of all children as well.

CHAPTER 11

Mainstreaming:

Some Basis for Caution

Robert Stannard

One of the few pleasures remaining to a superintendent in the 1970s that is not illegal, immoral, or otherwise prohibited by the Education Code or Title V, is fantasizing. Imagine with me, if you will, a World War II movie. Brian Donleavy, with a trim moustache and a neat uniform, is the general, probably located in a beautiful villa several hundred miles away from the theater of action. Much nearer the front in a bombed-out abbey or farm house, Colonel Broderick Crawford, gruff and hard, occupies a position of command. And finally, right in the thick of things, in the front line, covered with dirt and dust and showing the wear of sixty or seventy hours of consecutive combat, without a cigarette, carrying his carbine in one hand, is Lieutenant John Wayne. Now for dialogue. The General to the Colonel: "Ike says we must slow their attack and I want you to throw everything you've got at them. It's crucial. Don't fail." The Colonel, in the next scene, to the Lieutenant: "Old blood and guts says we've got to stop them and stop them we will. I know your company has led every attack since D-Day. You're short a man and the new recruits are green and incompetent, but damn it, John, you've got to do the job." Third scene: Lieutenant John Wayne is right in the foxhole yelling at his men over the roar of the battle: "The old man says we've got to do it again. We've got to stop them. We've got to destroy their armored division, encircle their infantry, and capture Romania. We can do it." About one hundred and ten minutes later, they will have done it, with pauses for only a few occasional flashbacks to the farm scene or back to Paris or for appropriate directions in an otherwise very active movie.

This fantasy was prompted by my thinking about some of the irresponsible and some of the unreasonable claims put forth for mainstreaming and the Master Plan in California. The generals and colonels and lieutenants in education, I believe, are running a very real risk of winning a battle or two but perhaps losing the war. They will be losing gains made in a hundred years of struggle in California. There are very few—and I know of none personally—who disagree with the concept of integrating handicapped and non-handicapped children. Benefits accrue to both. In these situations, it's a valuable experience. Integration increases the positive interaction between the handicapped and non-handicapped learner. However, we cannot help recall, with some degree of shame and guilt, our society's efforts to segregate portions of its population on reservations, internment centers, asylums, and racially segregated schools.

I'm not sure, however, that that treatment was any less harmful than its aftermath. Was the American Indian any better off when he entered the mainstream? For him, it meant moving to a large city, living a life of rejection and isolation once again. Is the black or Chicano, when thrust into a hostile environment, treated any less humanely than he was in a segregated school in the ghetto or in the barrio? Will it be different for the retarded child or the palsied child? In some cases, we have created institutions that have thrust upon them new freedoms not previously experienced. I believe, in each of these cases, that we have neglected rejected, isolated, and dehumanized those whom we were trying to help. It seems to follow, then, that mainstreaming is an effort that will avoid the evils of isolation and neglect and will provide humane and enlightened treatment. I will leave it to others to validate the benefits of mainstreaming. Rather, I would like to discuss with you some of the problems that John Wayne and his men, the school districts in our state, will face in defeating the armored units encircling the infantry and in finally capturing Romania.

May I share first with you a comment by Edward

Martin, Deputy Commissioner of Education of the Handicapped, who last year said:

> I'm concerned today about the pell mell and, I fear, naive mad dash into mainstreaming children based upon our hopes for better things for them. First, it is a question of attitudes, fears, anxieties, and possibly over-rejection which may face handicapped children, not just from their schoolmates but from the adults in the schools. If the majority of handicapped children, the mildly and moderately retarded, the children with behavioral disorders, the children with language and learning problems, the children with orthopedic difficulties are to be spending much or most of their time in regular classrooms, there must be a massive effort to work with their regular teachers. We cannot just instruct them in the pedagogy of special education but must share their feelings, understand their fears and provide them with the assistance and materials. In short, we must assure their success.

The massive effort to which he refers is not unknown to me. For three years we were privileged in North Sacramento to undertake a Title III program that we labeled the Model Class program. Briefly, the project, which began in 1969, has as its objective the return of the majority of educable retarded and educationally handicapped children to the regular classroom. It should be emphasized that by "regular classroom" we do not mean what is often accepted as regular. The entire structure of the classroom must be modified, not only to accommodate the exceptional child, but also to provide individualized instruction more effectively to all children in the class. To return the special child to the regular class that rejected him in the first place would be a serious error. The original design of the project called for the placement of six exceptional children, three EMR and three EH who had previously been in self-contained special classes, in a third-grade classroom. The addition to these children of twenty-two regular-class children brought the class to twenty-eight. A teacher aide was added to bring the adult/pupil ratio to 14:1. The plan called for adding a fourth-grade class during the second year of the project and a fifth-grade class during the third year, all with similar ratios.

The instructional pattern called for learning centers with increasingly heavy emphasis on individualized instruction and precision teaching. The in-service component of the ten teachers each year included workshops, development of materials, testing materials, and one week of instructional practice in one of the model classrooms. The project was a success. When results were compared with control classes of both handicapped and non-handicapped children, the handicapped children with the regular-class children did as well or significantly better academically than their isolated counterparts. With respect to behavior, there was either a comparable gain or the handicapped children in the model class improved more. Finally, with respect to attitudinal change, the handicapped students in the model classroom did better.

The results of the three-year project were encouraging. They suggest that educators might maintain the special child within regular class programs and still provide an effective learning situation for all children. However, modifications in regular-class procedures must be made to accommodate these children. Such modifications tend to benefit not only the special child but the majority of children in the classroom as well. The normal child does not seem to suffer from living and working with his less fortunate peers. Indeed, in many cases, the special child becomes difficult to find in this modified environment and the labels we have pinned on him tend to fade. The concern one frequently hears expressed is that returning the special child to the regular classroom will somehow dilute the educational program for the non-handicapped child. This did not occur in our situation. The results show that the non-handicapped children in this program improved as much or more as the control groups in other classes where special children were not being taught.

With this real experience in hand, why should I be raising any doubts about mainstreaming? Didn't we prove that it worked, that benefits accrue to all? What more could the generals and the colonels and lieutenants want? Our experience was dependent upon extensive outside funding and utilization of truly exceptional teachers and consultants.

We experienced the benefits of the Hawthorne effect, and the project encompassed only hand-picked volunteer project people and in-service participants. It wasn't the real world. It was not intended to be. The purpose was to test whether integration or mainstreaming using EMR or EH children in specially engineered classrooms could result in their functioning as well as they could have in their segregated classes—and to test the effects on the remainder of the class.

Having, I hope, established to some extent at least a practical base for further comment, let me list some of my concerns about implementing mainstreaming in California's public schools. First, to date, the legislature has not indicated a willingness to fund the Master Plan. It has provided only very limited funds for a few pilot projects. The past performance of our legislature does not suggest either an acknowledgment of or a willingness to make the necessary massive commitment of additional funds that I believe are essential to the success of the Master Plan. Several years ago, here in California, we were very pleased to see the state legislature adopt Senate Bill 90, which contained a provision that the legislature would not mandate any new programs without providing for their funding. But he who writes the law can just as easily bend the law. In the past few years, bill after bill has been introduced, and many have been passed into law, which do require additional funds. But the legislature, in each instance, with the power granted to it, has added at the end of each of those laws a statement that, in its opinion, no additional cost accrues to the local school district. This absolves the legislature of all responsibility to fund the mandated program. I have no confidence that adequate funding will be forthcoming from the legislature. But I may have made a mistake in listing financing first, because I certainly don't believe that it is the major problem facing us.

Second, in our model program we invested a great deal of time and energy working each year with ten hand-picked volunteer teachers in an in-service program attempting first to change attitudes toward handicapped children, second to learn the skills of individualized instruction, and third to gain the commitment to express the new attitudes and skills in their own classrooms in the future. We succeeded, but only to a limited extent. Mainstreaming, which would potentially affect every teacher in California, will not—cannot—succeed without a massive change in attitudes and skills. If you will, think for just a minute that most teachers in California and, I'm afraid, too many teachers now in training in our institutions have been instructed, have been very well taught, have been convinced, that one of their professional duties is to identify, locate, and assist in the placement of exceptional children in special classes. We have been trained to exclude, not to accept and include. And, not surprisingly, this training has brought its own rewards. It reduces class size, maybe not permanently but at least temporarily. And more importantly it eases the instructional burden by removing non-conforming individuals. Frankly, I fail to see any practical reason for a regular classroom teacher to accept mainstreaming. Just the opposite. I see many reasons, admittedly very selfish ones, to oppose it.

Third, and speaking of teachers, we tend to assume that those at present in special education wholehartedly support mainstreaming and the Master Plan. I've found just the opposite since the Master Plan has become a known commodity, a topic of discussion in teachers' rooms and in in-service meetings. Our special-class teachers are proud of the job they're doing now, and I believe rightly so. Integration of exceptional children into normal classes to the extent that the abilities and acceptance are there, is commonplace now in most special classes. The feeling of guilt and shame isn't a burden to most of our special-class teachers now; they're proud of the job they are doing. They have had success in moving children from special-class placements back into regular placements as they move through the grades and through junior and senior high school. They have had success, not total, but certainly success that we can be proud of, in moving handicapped children, who perhaps cannot succeed well academically, into the work force in our state. They have a lot of improvements to make, but I don't think they need to be ashamed of the efforts that they've made to date. Mainstreaming is a threat to these teachers. It changes their role and the professional status they've aspired to and that they're successful in at the present time.

Fourth, although the development of the Master Plan

included parent participation at the state level and, I assume, parent agreement, I believe that there will be increasing opposition by parents to the loss of special classes. It will be sparked and kindled, unfortunately, by incidents of rejection by the normal students and their parents, by teachers and administrators, by secretaries and bus drivers and cooks. Again, we will reap the results of years of work by educators, but primarily by parents, in creating these special classes; and to that harvest of special classes and special training, mainstreaming represents a blight. It is not the goal that parent groups have been working for.

Fifth, if our experience is valid, individualized instruction in the mainstreamed classroom is essential—absolutely essential. Though every district in California, probably in the United States, honestly believes it individualizes, even casual observation indicates that it just isn't true. Retraining is difficult. Retraining without intrinsic motivation is a challenge to every in-service coordinator and every teacher-training institution. Not only are the skills of individualizing needed but positive attitudes toward individuals must be taught.

This may be a good time to pause to dispel a myth that may be growing in your, the reader's, mind. Am I a typical superintendent who came up through the coaching ranks, more comfortable with budgets than with people, thinking fondly of the past and holding desperately to the status quo and concerned about not taking risks? Well, I hope not. That is an all-too-common stereotype that I think has less and less basis in reality. I honestly believe that I don't fit that stereotype, nor do many of my colleagues. I had the opportunity a few years ago to serve as the principal at a school for orthopedically handicapped blind and deaf children. At the same time, I supervised a countywide program that included not only those disabilities but the educable and the trainable retarded programs. We believed in, and practiced, extensive integration. It was the hallmark of the program in Marin County. I'm sure that it still is. Perhaps, I make this diversion to reassure myself, but I must share my concerns.

Let me list a few more concerns which may, in the long run, prove to be important but difficult to overcome. Collective bargaining is a reality in California, and recent court decisions, which are a reality and occupy a position as the law of the land in California, place educational policy and programing on the bargaining table. What will be the position of the CTA, the AFT, the school boards, individual teacher associations, individual negatiators, on the issue of mainstreaming? Will it be used as a trade-off item to gain another goal—a *quid quo pro*? And by whom? Who will be speaking for the children and their parents in this process?

Lack of trained resource teachers is a problem now being met by many institutions aroudn California. But why do we imagine that a special-education teacher now can be or wants to be taught a new set of skills that include the new dimension of working with a variety of other adults, not merely a variety of other children? How difficult will it be to understand the wide range of learning styles represented by the wide range of handicapped children appearing in the mainstreamed classroom? And finally, who will assume responsibility for changing attitudes among the normal children so that mainstreaming is a positive blending of children, not a confrontation or, even worse, rejection? Will it be the parent, the principal, the resource teacher—or the regular classroom teacher? Who will assume this responsibility? I believe that much of the battle for the Master Plan by the legislature, the State Department of Education, and district boards and administrators is being waged on movie sets for public viewing. It is good entertainment with a high rating but is devoid of much reality. But fantasy or not, there is a problem to be faced. The Master Plan is reality and its objectives are laudable.

I'm sure that there are others who are far more knowledgeable and insightful as regards mainstreaming, but I have several suggestions. The first is a very simple one to state, but perhaps a very difficult one to implement: Recognize the problems that face us. Too often, we have moved into new fields of endeavor while avoiding the problems. They don't go away. Quite often, when ignored, they become cancerous, eating at the core of the problem we're trying to solve.

Second, I would urge those in decision-making positions to slow down. Not to stop—but to slow down. I believe it can be better, and I think we should work on improving the quality of our special classes as they exist. Let's allow time for local communities and local school staffs to develop attitudes and skills and to reorganize priorities.

Third, good intentions are seldom enough. Slick gimmicks by the legislature to avoid paying the bills only create greater problems. More dollars are needed—many more. The pilot projects need to be more adequately funded, and mandated programs must be fully funded.

Fourth, let's learn from these pilot programs. Let's develop a dissemination program, encourage good research, and provide for visitations. Let's be big enough to accept failures in some pilot programs, rather than hiding them. Certainly, those in other fields of endeavor learn from their failures. We have them; we should learn from them. It reminds me of a question that was asked of Thomas Edison when he was in the process of inventing the light bulb. One of his co-workers said, "Aren't you terribly discouraged? You've tried two hundred different materials for the filament and none of them work." Edison is supposed to have replied, "I've eliminated two hundred that I need not look at again." He saw that failures are really a step toward a solution, and I think we must have that attitude as we attempt to improve education in California.

Fifth, and finally, education is a people enterprise. Provide mandate if you must—wide community involvement at the local school and community levels. Not a blue-ribbon statewide committee, but local people, in the planning, implementation, and evaluation of the Master Plan. I have a great deal of confidence that, when enough people work together cooperatively, positive results will occur.

A postscript: let's stop thinking of it as a Master Plan. The label connotes an authoritarian pronouncement from on high. Let's think of it as an opportunity for local districts to increase the educational opportunities for all children by capitalizing on the untapped aspirations and potentials of the handicapped child. Perhaps the Master Plan, especially the mainstreaming component, offers a new opportunity. *Special education is in a unique position to serve as developmental capital to upgrade the effectiveness of the total public education effort.* Enter into cooperative competition with regular education to act as an advocate for those children, handicapped or not, who fall out or are squeezed out of the educational mainstream. This impact should and, I think, will affect every aspect of education.

About the Authors

PATRICK A. O'DONNELL, EdD, coeditor of this volume, is chairman of the Department of Special Education at San Francisco State University. Author of numerous books and journal articles and coauthor of *Teaching the Physically Handicapped* (in press), he serves on many advisory boards and professional organizations in the field of special education.

RICHARD BANCROFT, LLM, is a superior court judge of Alameda County (California). He has served on the faculties of Dominican College (San Rafael, California), San Francisco State University, and California State University at Hayward, and is a frequent lecturer on the topic of the legal rights of exceptional children.

BARBARA KEOGH, PhD, is a professor of special education at UCLA and is director of the university's Special Education Research Program. A certified psychologist in the state of California, she has been editor and consulting editor of several professional journals in the fields of school psychology and learning disabilities.

MAYNARD REYNOLDS, PhD, is a professor of psychoeducational studies and chairman of the Department of psychoeducational studies at the University of Minnesota.

ASA G. HILLIARD, EdD, is Dean of the School of Education at San Francisco State University. He is currently a member of the Executive Committee Board of the American Association of Colleges for Teacher Education.

ARMANDO M. MENOCAL, III is a San Francisco attorney. He is chairperson of the San Francisco Bar Association's Committee of the Judiciary and Section on Public Interest Law, and is a member of the State Bar of California's Committee of Bar Examiners.

JOANNE CONDAS RABIN, JD, is Deputy Attorney General of California, and represents California's various health, welfare, and education agencies. She is a member of the U. S. Supreme Court Bar and the California State Bar.

LEO CAIN, PhD, is president of California State University at Dominguez Hills. Coauthor of two books, *TMR School Competency Scales* and *Cain-Levine Social Competency Scale.* He is also a member of the Task Force on Handicapped Children's Project; a past national president of the Council for Exceptional Children; and a consultant and former member of the President's Committee on Retardation.

CHARLES MEISGEIER, PhD, is a professor of curriculum and instruction and chairman of the Special Education Program at the University of Houston. He is the author of two books, *The Process of Special Education Administration* and *The Doubly Disadvantaged.*

HUGH MCKENZIE, PhD, is a professor of special education at the University of Vermont, and is director of the university's Center for Special Education.

ROBERT H. BRADFIELD, PhD, coeditor of this volume, is an associate professor of special education at San Francisco State University. Chief consultant for the North Sacramento Mainstream Project, he is the author of two books, *Behavior Modification: The Human Effort* and *Behavior Modification of Learning Disabilities.*

ROBERT STANNARD, MA, is superintendent of the Morgan Hills (California) Unified School District. He has lectured on varied aspects of school administration and has published papers in several professional journals.